P9-APL-649

# What Do I Want?

## ANNIE CHAPMAN

Vessels of Honor Resources
S & A FAMILY, INC.
MADISON, TN 37116

©1999 by Annie Chapman
Edited by Steve Chapman and Amy Carlson
Cover and print design by Maksimowicz Design
Back cover photo: Dave Hawkins

———

All scripture quotations are taken from the NEW KING JAMES VERSION
and the NEW AMERICAN STANDARD BIBLE

———

All rights reserved. No part of this publication may be reproduced,
stored in a retrieval system, or transmitted in any form by
any means, electronic, mechanical, photocopy, recording or
otherwise without the prior written permission of the
publisher, except as provided by USA copyright law.

———

Printed in the USA

———

Library of Congress Cataloging-in-Publication Data
Chapman, Annie
What Do I Want?
ISBN 0-9653274-3-4

# What Do
# I Want?

*I dedicate this book to the loving memory
of my parents
Sylvia Alice Eckard Williamson
and
Ney Rene Williamson, Sr.
They were faithful to one another
as marriage partners for fifty-two years.
Now they are friends forever.
They are desperately missed.*

# CONTENTS

# INTRODUCTION

I'll never forget the evening I took my younger sister out to dinner for her birthday. As the mother of four children, with the oldest only five, she definitely needed a break. Some of you who have grown children may have forgotten what it's like to be the mother of little ones. Let me simply remind you. Basically, kids suck the brains right out of your head. The truth was, we both needed a break and we were especially excited about getting to spend some time together, just the two of us.

As we were leaving, her husband was standing on the porch. He held the baby in his arms and the other three children were climbing up his pant leg as though he were a ladder. His face revealed the horror he was feeling. He looked like a "deer in the headlights." (I felt sorry for him, which honestly surprised me.)

All the way to the car, my sister was calling back words of love and comfort to her family. "Mommy loves her babies. Don't worry, Honey. I won't be that late. Be good for Daddy!" Then she went into some really gushy mommy dialect. "I wuv ooo! Mommy wuvs ooo!!" She was throwing kisses until the moment she closed the car door. Once inside, out of earshot of her crying children, she then looked over at me and said with a slight mischievous growl in her voice, **"FLOOR IT!!"**

Like my sister, who obviously needed a rest from the rigors of her important job as a young wife and mother, I recall feeling the same way. I would cry out to the Lord, "Where are the older women who are supposed to be teaching those of us who are younger how to survive motherhood?" One day, years later, as I was praying this same prayer, I felt the Lord speak gently to my heart, "You are the older woman." It is on that basis that I humbly offer the insights contained in these pages.

# CHAPTER
# ONE

I DID INDEED

ASK A LOT OF QUESTIONS WHEN I WAS IN

MY TEENS AND EARLY ADULT YEARS, AND,

AMAZINGLY ENOUGH, I'M STILL ASKING THE

SAME ONES. BUT OF ALL THE QUESTIONS

I ASKED, MY FAVORITE ONE IS,

**"WHAT DO I WANT?"**

# What I Want

I am a baby boomer who is in the middle of being middle-aged; that is, if I live to be really old. I've probably lived as many days as I have left to live. There's nothing wrong with being middle-aged, if you're on the correct side of the middle. The problem I'm having is, I'm on the far side of the equation. I'm on the side of mid-life where everything starts to fall apart.

Gravity is a wonderful thing. It keeps the glass on the table and the chair held down on the floor. Gravity pulls other things down as well. I talked to a beautiful eighty year old woman who told me she had all the same body parts she had at twenty. The only problem was, they were all in a different place. Another woman said she was in a crowd and was very upset when she thought someone had pinched her behind. But then she realized they had just accidentally stepped on it!

One day I was watching one of those info-mercials where they were selling face cream. The women kept talking about trying to get rid of those "fine lines." Though no one was around to hear my reaction, I went ahead and said it out loud just for my ears. "Hey! The fine lines are not the problem, ladies. It's the lines you can park a jeep in! That's the problem!"

Being a baby boomer made me a part of the generation that was always asking questions. Some of you ladies have white hair because you raised one of those irritating young people. We were always asking questions like, "WHO AM I? WHERE DID I COME FROM?" and, "WHY AM I HERE?"

My mother was a very wise woman. Whenever her children started asking those grandiose questions, she very keenly told us, "Go on down to the courthouse, they have all that information on file down there. They can tell you who you are and where you came from. But as far as the business of why you're here, you'll just have to figure that one out for yourself."

I did indeed ask a lot of questions when I was in my teens and early adult years, and, amazingly enough, I'm still asking the same ones. But of all the questions I asked, my favorite one is, **"WHAT DO I WANT?"**

There are five days of the year that I really love: VALENTINE'S DAY, MOTHER'S DAY, MY ANNIVERSARY, MY BIRTHDAY, AND CHRISTMAS. The reason I look forward to these special days is because that's when my family asks me, "WHAT DO YOU WANT?" Ah! What a sweet sound that inquiry is to my ears. At that moment I have all the permission I ever need to whisper to myself, "What do I want?" I love it!

You would think that once a person matures to the mid-life years as I have, those questions asked unreservedly in the 1960's would have been thrown away with the lava lamps and the black lights. However, they still remain. And I've discovered that my middle-aged friends are still asking those questions as well.

One day I was having lunch with some of those friends. (It is terribly sad, by the way, when I realize how infrequently we are able to share with one another. No one has time to get together, because we all have so many responsibilities. Nonetheless, on this day we were finally having some time together). We all took turns whining about our lives. There were complaints about messy, unruly children; inconsiderate, overworked spouses; demanding employers; disconnected family and friends; aging, ailing parents; out-of-touch churches; and of course, our tired, over-weight, out-of-shape bodies. It was an exhilarating time of fellowship.

As I was driving away, reflecting on our time together, I was amazed at how overwhelmed we all seemed to be. I thought of the scripture found in Matthew 11:29. "Come unto me, all who are weary and heavy-laden (works to exhaustion) and I will give you rest. Take my yoke upon you, and learn from Me, for I am gentle and humble in heart; and you shall find rest for your souls. For my yoke is easy (pleasant), and My load is light."

Thinking back over the time with my friends that day, I was faced with the reality that the conversations I had just witnessed did not line up with that particular scripture. I realized that the burdens described that afternoon were not easy or pleasant. The loads that my friends and I were carrying did not seem light at all.

Whenever I think of the many demands on my life, I often recall the old Ed Sullivan shows. I remember watching those broadcasts as a child, which is a rather depressing thought, considering how long ago they were aired. Now understand, I'm not talking about the reruns on cable, I'm talking about the real thing. (Just a little side bar, Steve and I used to point out to our children the various TV programs we watched when we were young. Of course, all of them were in black and white, an era missed by our living-color-kids. One day one of the children asked, "When was color invented?" They assumed since all the shows we watched in our childhood were in black and white, as well as the pictures of us as children, there were no colors when we were young. Don't we have smart children?)

Anyway, one of my favorite acts on the Ed Sullivan show was the juggler who would come onto the stage and start twirling plates on long, reed-like sticks. He would start a plate spinning, then another, and another, until the stage was filled with spinning plates. He would then run frantically back and forth trying to keep the plates from falling. It was exhausting to watch as a plate, out of his view, would start to wobble and begin to fall. The audience would yell to him and he would run to the rescue.

That juggler's act is what my life looks like. I have so many responsibilities and people depending on me, I feel like I'm furiously running back and forth trying to keep my life from crashing to the floor. I have children who are in college who still need me. I have a husband, that I adore, who needs my attention from time to time. I have our work on behalf of families that requires extensive travel, writing, and preparations. Also, I have friends who have needs. I want to spend time with them, but I can't. We would love to be more involved with our church. And, in the past few months, we have felt a desire to assist in the founding of a new ministry to couples, especially pastors and their wives. Everything we want and need to do is very important. Yet, it is extremely difficult to work everything in to its proper place of priority.*

With all the demands on my life, I find it necessary to come back to my original question and once again ask myself, "WHAT DO I WANT?"

During the course of these few pages, I'm going to share some things that I have concluded I really do desire (actually, I desperately NEED).

# CHAPTER
## TWO

BEFORE I CAN HAVE

WHAT I WANT IN LIFE,

I MUST FIRST ALLOW CHRIST

TO HAVE WHAT HE WANTS

FROM ME.

# I Want to Be Christlike

Since I am a Christian, it may seem logical I would begin my list of wants with something religious. That is not at all the reason I say I want to be Christlike. This is not just a religious nicety. Coming to know Christ literally saved my life.

I grew up in rural West Virginia. In the early years as a child, we were a non-churched family. But one day a preacher came to our house. Mom invited him in to the front room while she went into the kitchen to get him a glass of water. I was left in the front room with the preacher. He knelt down and showed me a picture. I'm not sure where he got it, perhaps out of his wallet, but it was the classic painting of Jesus standing at the door, knocking. He then told me something that would change the life of a dirty-faced, bare-foot, little girl nearly five years old. He pointed to the picture of Jesus and simply said, "That man loves you." I remember thinking, "If He loves me, then I love Him." I was unaware that I was fulfilling the scripture, I John 4:19, "We love Him because He first loved us." The knowledge of Christ's love for me would become the divine vehicle that would carry me over the difficult years ahead.

Not long after the preacher's visit, there were devastating events that happened to me which caused me to be a very unhappy child. (I will share more about this later in the book.) I spent a lot of my childhood wanting to die. I would go out on the hillside and pray, "If there is really a God, then kill me and get me out of my misery. Don't make me live and be so unhappy." No matter how sad and depressed I would get, however, I could not shake the image of Jesus at that door. God was gracious to advance me the awareness of His love. That, along with the loving support of my wonderful parents, sustained me during those horrible years of despair.

It would be much later that I would hear the rest of the story of Christ. I learned that not only did Jesus love me, but He loved me enough to die for me. When I was eighteen, I made the "great exchange." I exchanged my desire to die for God's generous gift of eternal life. When I gave my wounded heart to Jesus, He gave me a brand new one. And, along with that renewal, He took away the desire and the need to die. I truly believe, had I not come to know Christ, I would not be alive today. I could not have gone on feeling the way I did. So to say, "I want to be Christlike," is for me, to live.

You may be feeling that same kind of despair. No one would know it to look at you, but like it was for me, death has a grip on your heart. This may be a very sad secret that you harbor alone. Perhaps something terrible has happened to you that causes you to be depressed and unhappy. I need to tell you some good news. "You don't have to live like that!" Jesus can take away your desire to die and give you the reason to live. If you feel like something is missing from your life, you are correct. All of us were designed with a God-shaped need in our lives. Only He can fill that place. Don't allow another day to go by without letting Jesus illuminate the deep, dark regions in your heart with His light and life. Nothing else can fill that void. I tried overeating to make me feel complete; it only made me fat. I tried over achieving to make me feel whole; it only made me tired. I tried buying pretty things to make me feel happy; it only left me broke. I tried loving people; they left me disappointed.

God designed us so that nothing can fill our emptiness except Him. He is jealous for our love and devotion and He loves us too much to let us find a substitute for His perfect love (Deuteronomy 6:13-15).

So, before I can have what I want in life, I must first allow Christ to have what He wants from me. First and foremost, I want to be Christlike.

# CHAPTER
# THREE

As we were walking into

the bathroom on that hot day in Texas,

I realized that if we didn't keep

a balance, we were going to end up

with a serious mess on our hands.

The same is true of our lives.

Ladies, if we fail to keep a balance as

wives and mothers, we too will end up

with a mess on our hands.

# I Want To Be Coordinated

———

Somehow, I want to find a balance in my life as I juggle all the demands on me. Two important areas where I desperately want coordination are in my responsibilities as a wife and mother.

One day I was faced with a very tangible example of my need for balance. I want to retell one of my favorite stories that happened when our children were very small.*

Steve and I have traveled together in a singing ministry on behalf of families, with our children, Nathan and Heidi, since 1975. (The kids are now twenty-two and nineteen years old and both are in college at the time of this writing.) We started taking our children along even before they were born. It was quite a challenge to do the regular things required for child rearing, especially while traveling. For instance, I would breast feed our baby, and then we would present a musical concert. I could only hope that we would finish singing before my milk would let down again. Oh! The glamour of it all! Before long, the children were weaned, but then it was time to do the dreaded potty training phase.

We traveled in a little, un-airconditioned van, with

no toilet facilities. In order to keep life sane and to avoid the nasty service station bathrooms, we bought a little plastic potty chair, and set it in the middle of the van. One day while in Texas, we forgot that the potty chair was behind the van and we accidentally backed over it. So, we had to purchase a new one. The children wanted to make it feel welcomed so they used it a lot. I mean…A LOT!

By the time we got to the church where we were going to sing that night, the pot was like a bubbling cauldron. The intense southwest heat only added to the pungent situation. So, arriving three or four hours before the concert gave us ample time to dump and sanitize the potty. Now, the decision was "who" was going to do this dastardly deed. Steve and I decided we needed to use our standard way of making decisions like these. We flipped for it. Unfortunately, for me, the coin did not land my way. I lost…big time!

I took the whole potty chair into the church with me. I maneuvered the door with my hip and elbow and swung myself into the church. The old potty chair had a bar across the back that kept the pot in place. The new one did not have that feature. As I swung myself into the church, I was surprised when the full pot flew out of the chair and landed, contents down, right inside the entrance. It looked as though I had opened up the door and deliberately dumped "you know what" on the carpet.

I've had some bad things happen to me in my life,

but this was right up there with the worst. I thought to myself, "This would be a good time for the Lord to come back." I waited and He didn't. I really wanted the earth to open up and swallow me. In my panic, I looked down and realized that there was a piece of plastic lying on the floor. What a relief! The pot had divinely landed right in the middle of that plastic.

Off to my right there was a teenager sweeping the steps. He had witnessed the whole fiasco. Standing there stunned, I screamed for him to come over and help me. We very gingerly picked up the plastic by the corners and carefully walked it into the men's restroom. There was a reason, by the way, that I chose the men's bathroom. By the look on that poor kid's face, if I had tried taking him into the ladies' restroom, I think it might have pushed him over the edge. There is, to this day, a young man in Texas to whom I feel strangely bonded.

As we were walking into the bathroom on that hot day in Texas, I realized that if we didn't keep a balance, we were going to end up with a serious mess on our hands. The same is true of our lives. Ladies, if we fail to keep a balance as wives and mothers, we too will end up with a real mess on our hands.

# CHAPTER
## FOUR

EVEN THOUGH THERE ARE MANY

RESPONSIBILITIES AS WIVES AND MOTHERS,

WE MUST NOT MAKE THE MISTAKE

OF CONSTANTLY PUTTING OUR HUSBANDS

ON THE BACK BURNER.

# I Want To Be A Coordinated Wife

One afternoon I was talking to a friend of mine who had small children. She was totally overwhelmed. As we were talking on the phone, she began describing her previous day. She said that it was 2 o'clock in the afternoon before she got out of her bed clothes. She was still in her night gown, not because she was lying around all day, but she had not found enough time to even slip into a pair of sweats. It had been a terrible day; everything had gone wrong. The children had acted like absolute animals, her house was a wreck, and she looked horrible. Her husband came home that evening, sneaked up behind her, and started nuzzling on her neck. She wheeled around and met him nose to nose, and said, "Look, buddy, that's the last thing I need!"

Now, for some reason she didn't think he was just giving her one of those 8-12 meaningful, non-sexual touches that Gary Smalley talks about in his relationship seminars. She seemed to think that his little gesture meant "somebody else wants something from me."

I understood what she was talking about. I'm sure you do as well. Haven't we all had the kind of day she described when we gave all we had to give, yet it seemed our family still wanted more? I truly commiserated with her. However, as she related how she had reacted to her husband, I could see the words from Proverbs 14:1 scroll across my mind like the messages on the electronic marquee at our local bank. "A wise woman builds her house, but the foolish tears it down with her own hands."

Even though there are many responsibilities as wives and mothers, we must not make the mistake of constantly putting our husbands on the back burner. Of course, there will be those times when necessity demands that our attention be diverted away from our spouses and we would expect them to be adult about it. However, it is unfair to always be pushing our husbands aside.

As I continued talking to my friend, I thought about her husband's situation at work. He was a man with influence and status. I'm sure there were women around him who would have willingly made him feel loved and desirable. A wise woman will strive for a balance between the demands of her children and the needs of her husband, or visa-versa.

There are at least three areas to keep in mind as we relate to our husbands.

1. WORK AS A TEAM: Philippians 4:3 says, "Indeed, true comrade, I ask you also to help these women who have shared my struggle in the cause of the gospel, together with Clement also, and the rest of

my fellow workers (yoke fellows), whose names are in the book of life."

**Yoke fellows**—that's a good description of marriage. I like to think of the marriage union as two oxen in a yoke. The purpose of that device is to help a pair pull a load. There are two different scenarios that could apply to the yoke picture. One would be where the wife is out of the yoke and sitting on the wagon. She is a rather passive part of the marriage. She does not want to participate as an equal.

If she leaves her husband to do it all, and he makes all the decisions, then she is not responsible for a choice **when,** not **if,** it turns out to be wrong. It may look like submission to the rest of the world when she responds, "Yes, Dear, whatever you want, Dear." But really, it's not submission at all. It's just being a lazy coward.

The other scenario would be if she's out of the yoke, in front of the wagon, calling the shots. She has taken over and dominates the situation. Onlookers might say, "Oh! What a strong, independent woman!" However, I suggest that she is a woman driven by fear. A controlling person is someone who is afraid, too frightened to trust and to love. They fear that if they give up control, something might happen they don't like.

Love cannot grow in the soil of fear. Often we believe that hate is the opposite of love. Rather, fear is the opposite, because "Perfect love casts out fear."

(I John 4:18)

Being out of the yoke, either by sitting on the wagon or being a dominant controller, is an inaccurate picture of what God intended. Marriage is a partnership. Both husband and wife are to be pulling the load together. Only you know where you are in your marriage. What others may think is totally irrelevant. Only you know your heart. Are you a coward, blaming your husband for your unhappiness, your lack of success, your sense of worthlessness? Or are you a woman driven by fear and control?

One of the manifestations of fear is anger. Look at your life. Are you a person who is given to bouts of unprovoked hostility? If so, look for the areas in your life that are dominated by fear. God's perfect love, as it is worked out in your daily life, teaching you to trust Him, can deliver you from this anger and need to control. Being out of the yoke of partnership leads to discontentment, and disillusionment in a marriage. So…get back in the yoke.

Being a team player will yield far greater results in the life of a couple. I once heard about a horse pulling contest. The winning horse pulled 4,500 pounds. The runner up pulled 4,000 pounds. But then they put the horses together, and working side by side, they were able to pull over 12,000 pounds. We get so much more accomplished as a team, and as a family, if we pull together and stop competing against each other. Marriage is much more enjoyable when both are winning.

2. WATCH YOUR TONGUE: We find a warning against one of the greatest enemies of our marriage in James 3:2-10: "For we all stumble in many ways. If anyone does not stumble in what he says, he is a perfect man, able to bridle the whole body as well. Behold, the ships also, though they are so great and are driven by strong winds, are still directed by a very small rudder, wherever the inclination of the pilot desires. So also the tongue is a small part of the body, and yet it boasts of great things. Behold, how great a fire is set aflame by such a small fire! And the tongue is a fire, the very world of iniquity; the tongue is set among our members as that which defiles the entire body, and sets on fire the course of our life, and is set on fire by hell. For every species of beast and birds, or reptiles and creatures of the sea, is tamed, and has been tamed by the human race. But no one can tame the tongue; it is a restless evil and full of deadly poison. With it we bless our Lord and Father; and with it we curse men, who have been made in the likeness of God. From the same mouth come both blessing and cursing. My brethren, (my sisters) these things ought not to be this way."

I have a friend who told me about an argument she and her husband had. During the heat of the discussion he turned to her and said, "You can castrate a man with your tongue quicker than you can with a knife!" (I know all the men reading these words just flinched at the thought.) But ladies, this is true. We must make a pact with our tongues. We must be careful to restrain what we say and how we say it.

Possibly one of the best opportunities God gives a woman to practice talking to her spouse in a kind manner is found in the children she may have. We can be quick to say things to our kids that can cut them off at the knees. I recall a time when I was talking to Nathan about a mark he brought home when he was in the eighth grade. The previous year was a very difficult time for Nathan and me. I home schooled him in the 7th grade...and that is why he was attending regular school for the 8th grade. I decided I could be his mother or his teacher, but at that time, I dared not be both.

Although Nathan had always had excellent grades and tested well above his age group, for some reason he came home with a 65 on a math test. I was not pleased with his score and I let him know it. After pounding him with my words, he then proceeded to tell me that 65 was actually a large number of points. He said, "Just think about it, mom! SIXTY-FIVE. That's a lot!"

I continued to lambaste him. I informed him that he was not applying himself enough. I warned him that if he didn't start working harder to get an education, he would end up homeless, sleeping under bridges. The unsanitary conditions would cause him to contract some deadly disease, then he'd have to come home and Mommy would have to take care of him. (All right, I admit I was a little melodramatic, but mothers have to revert to drastic measures to get through sometimes.) Nathan responded to my melodrama with a little of his own. Through tears of frustration, he said, "How would you like it, Mom, when you get to heaven, and you're standing before God, if He didn't say, 'Well done, thou good and faithful servant.' Instead, He says, 'You missed a spot.'"

Nathan's word picture was not wasted on me. For the first time in a long time, I saw the ugliness of my words and rough demeanor towards him. I had the ability and the inclination to cut my children down to size with my words and the tone of my voice. It was at that juncture that I took a good hard look at what I was saying to my children and how I was saying it. The truth is, I would never have used the same tone of voice or the lack of kindness with a neighbor, my pastor, or even the young man bagging my groceries. I became keenly aware of the scripture warning parents about provoking children to anger. Col. 3:21 cautions, "...do not exasperate your children, that they may not lose heart."

This warning to parents is just as applicable to wives! Are we using our tongues for sweetness or bitterness? We can speak words of harmony or harm to our husbands. The choice is ours.

WARNING ABOUT TV: I know that some of us feel we have little or no time with our husbands. With all of the demands of life, it is no wonder we end up feeling like a machine. We push a button and automatically do what has to be done. Throughout our day we go about in a robot-like stupor. However, when it comes to our relationship with our husbands, we need for the metal to fall away and tap into our humanness. Husbands and wives have a need for love and intimacy. With all the distractions around us, the home should be a reprieve.

A good place to start is by getting Leno and Letterman out of the bedroom. You may protest, "But, it would just cause a fight." Well, then fight. At least you'll be communicating with each other on some level. Too many couples don't have a clue about what each other is thinking or feeling, because they haven't taken the time to talk. The problems that have torn so many families apart could have been avoided if a sense of intimacy and knowledge of one another had been cultivated.

Of course, the Bible does not specifically talk about television or the influence such forms of entertainment may have on our homes. However, there are warnings that God gives which caution us about these dangers that could very well exist in our marriages.

In James 4:1-6, the passage asks, "Where do wars and fights come from among you? Do they not come from your desires for pleasure that war in your members?...Do you not know that friendship with the world is enmity with God? Whoever therefore wants to be a friend of the world makes himself an enemy of God…"

Our marriages will reflect what we have been feeding upon. (And remember, what we as parents accept in moderation, our children will embrace in excess). If we allow ungodly entertainment into our homes through network, cable, satellite dishes, and especially raw, unfiltered Internet access, and the like, our family will pay the price.

Pray with your husband about removing the TV from your bedroom. He may balk at the idea, but let me offer you just a little hint when approaching this subject with your spouse. Timing is everything. I don't need to tell you exactly when you should bring up this matter about the TV. However, at just the right moment you could say something like, "Honey, there are things that I would just love to say to you, and things I would love to do to you, but I'm just so distracted with that mean old television staring at me."

I can almost guarantee you, he'll get rid of that TV. If our husbands believe it is to their advantage to have this time together, they are more likely to take action. Take this need for a sanctified bedroom to God in prayer. You may be surprised at what He can do when we show Him how serious we are about loving and serving Him…and our husbands.

# CHAPTER
## FIVE

Today I freely admit,

God was so good and so wise

not to listen to me.

It was sheer selfishness

that caused me to shun the idea

of having children.

# I Want To Be A Coordinated Mother

Being born in 1951 and growing up in the "me" attitude of the sixties and early seventies, the idea of being a mother was never a role that I sought. I had been influenced by the feminist messages throughout college and didn't find the goal of the "white picket fence, with kids in the yard" to be my cup of tea. Though I became a Christian at eighteen, I still embraced some of the most ungodly attitudes of the feminist movement. Basically, I had a great disdain and hatred for men and children.

When Steve and I got married, I thought we had agreed to never have kids. Not many months after our wedding day, I mentioned the decision we had made. My intelligent husband said that he had no recollection of such a conversation. Not long after that, we attended a Bill Gothard Seminar in Atlanta, Georgia. While at the conference, there was teaching that covered the importance of a man's need to obediently follow the call of God in his life. Steve got a revelation…and I got pregnant.

Today I freely admit, God was so good and so wise to not listen to me. It was sheer selfishness that caused me to shun the idea of having children. I didn't want

the work, the worry, or the financial debt connected
with having little "cookie snatchers" running around
our duplex. Thank God! He looked beyond my sinful,
nasty self and gave us the most precious of all gifts.
Our children have turned out to be our best work. No
parents could love or be more proud of their children
than Steve and me. To the same degree of resistance I
had toward having children, that is the level to which
I now embrace the role of mother.

There are methods of mothering that we can adopt.
We can under-do it, or we can overdo it. I readily
admit that I fall into the latter category. I never wanted my children to have an unmet need.

When we brought Nathan home from the hospital,
I let him sleep on my stomach for the first week.
Thinking that he was used to hearing my heartbeat
and feeling the warmth of my body, I decided to wean
him away gradually. I'm not saying that this was such
a terrible idea, but I do know that neither of us was
getting much rest. So, I moved him into the bed
between Steve and me, even though I was afraid one
of us would roll over on him and hurt him.

Then one day a friend of mine came for a visit. She
had six children. I told her about my great idea of
keeping our newborn in bed with us. I expected her to
smile and pat me on the back. I was surprised, however, when she shamed me. She firmly admonished,
"You're tormenting your baby!" Her advice was revo-
lutionary. She said, "Put him in his crib and let him

get some rest. You look like you could use some, too!"
She went on to say, "If you don't let him learn to sleep
on his own, someday he'll come home from college
and say, 'Scoot over!'"

It was very difficult for me to even think about letting go and letting him out of my sight for the night.
As hard as it was to face, however, my friend helped
me see that it wasn't Baby Nathan that needed me
nearly as much as Mother Annie needed the baby. My
desire was innocent. I just wanted to know he was still
breathing. Reluctantly, I took my experienced friend's
advice and put our little bundle of restlessness in his
crib. Since that first long night without him, my body
has rested easier. But I must confess, my emotions have
continually dealt with the tiring process of letting go.

Heidi never cried for the first six weeks of her life.
**She didn't need to!** I would anticipate her every need
before she could even whimper. Steve began to believe
she was mute. But how untrue that theory was. Now,
19 years later, the only little girl in Steve's heart is away
at college. When her daddy sees the phone bill, he
realizes just how mistaken he was.

I was definitely guilty of overdoing it with both of
my children. Perhaps you are aware that the same ver-
dict could be handed down to you as a parent. The
truth is, we can "mother till we smother" our children.
This lop-sided method of parenting does have its
problems to overcome. But with the help of the Lord,
wise and seasoned friends and family, and eventually,

the assistance of time and distance, we will find coordination as a mother. But there is another side to this coin.

There are two philosophies floating around this nation that I find absolutely alarming when it comes to the relationship between moms and their children. First of all, it seems that in the minds of far too many parents, children are just an accessory of some kind. It appears that some couples want to have children only because they make such cute Christmas card pictures. They want the fun and the novel part of having kids but they are unwilling to accept the weighty responsibility of raising and caring for them on a daily basis.

This pervasive attitude of "I want to have a baby, but there is no way I'm going to limit my life by staying home to take care of it" is setting the stage for the collapse of our modern culture. We are not going to survive another generation of children who have never been nurtured and cared for.

We are paying a high price for the socially acceptable neglect that our children have suffered under the "day-care" mentality of this materialistic society. In 1950, adults committed serious crimes at a rate of 215 times the rate of children's serious crimes. (Those under the age of 14 are classified as children and serious crimes are defined as murder, rape, aggravated assault, and armed robbery.) There were only 170 children arrested in 1950 for serious crimes. By 1960, adult serious crimes were committed only eight to one

times that of children's crimes. The ratio went from
215-to-1, to 8-to-1 in ten years. By 1980 the rate was
five to one. So between 1950 and 1980, there was an
11,000 percent increase in crimes committed by children ages fourteen and under. When you consider the
heinous crimes by kids in very recent times, it would
be obvious to us all that our children are not doing
well without the daily guidance of loving, praying parents.

The human child is the most fragile of the mammal
infants, requiring more than a "kennel-care" type of
system. As a parent, you will more than likely be able
to find someone who will, if you pay them enough,
agree to feed, clothe, diaper, and make sure the child
is at least alive at the close of the day. However, **you
cannot pay someone to love your child.**

As wives who are busy and tired, and overworked,
we would never think of hiring a prostitute to come
into our home and "take care" of our husband's needs.
The element of love would be missing. If the idea of a
"wife for hire" sounds foolish, it is just as insane to
believe a "mom for hire" could really love our children. They may meet the basic needs, but where is the
mother's love that soothes the very spirit of a child,
that calms their fears, and feeds them with an assur-
ance that they belong to a family? The children won't
find that kind of attention in a "village!" There, they
only find confusion and unnecessary competition for
affection and attention. In their mother's arms is true

comfort.

John 10:11-14 says, "I am the good Shepherd. The good Shepherd gives His life for the sheep. But a hireling, he who is not the shepherd, one who does not own the sheep, sees the wolf coming and leaves the sheep and flees; and the wolf catches the sheep and scatters them. The hireling flees because he is a hireling and does not care about the sheep. I am the good Shepherd; and I know My sheep, and am known by My own."

Shining the light of the concept in this passage on the picture of moms and children makes a truth perfectly clear. No one you employ will ever love and care for them the way you would, nor the way they should be cared for. The person who is hired will flee when trouble comes. Why? Because your children are not their little lambs. It's as simple as that!

As a footnote to the concern we should show regarding "who" is watching the little ones, I must inject a warning that is fitting to this technical age in which we live. If you are permitting your young ones to be "babysat" by your computer, please be aware of the silicon wolves that stalk your children. If you have a PC that is linked to the Internet, but does not have some type of filter that blocks access to chat rooms and other dangerous sites, then you are insane.

I have a close friend who had taken the necessary precautions. She was the only one who knew the password, and her three boys could not get on line unless she secretly typed it in. In this way, she knew they could not gain access to the Internet when she wasn't at home.

There were term papers and school work that needed to be done. She gave in and let them have the password with the intentions of changing it when she got home. A few days went by before she did it. Finally, she went to the computer to change the secret code. Before doing so, she decided to take a look at the Internet sites the 12 year old had used for his research. What she found was devastating. The sexual perversion was so hideous that she went straightway to the bathroom and threw up. It was all extremely perverted and horrible. She couldn't even let her husband see what their young son had been into. She told me that it was obvious that normal sex was not even a part of the situation. It became apparent to her that in these days, normal, heterosexual sex is considered boring. If it isn't sick, it isn't stimulating.

I informed my friend of the Internet service carrier we use that provides the necessary blocking and encouraged her to subscribe to something similar. I urge all parents to do the same. If it is not done, I believe that giving our kids free access to the entire realm of the Internet is the same as handing them a box-full of scorpions to use as toys!

The second errant philosophy concerning mothers and children is the idea that kids want their mothers to be happy. We are led to believe that our children are concerned with our sense of well-being, our sense of accomplishment, and our self-esteem. My response to this nonsense is, "HOGWASH!!"

I am now going to tell you the truth. Our kids don't care if we're happy! They are concerned with **their** sense of well-being, **their** comfort, and **their** security. And, there's a good reason for their attitude. They are children!

Somehow, we have it all backwards. We expect children to think like adults and we excuse adults who act like children. It is indeed a mixed up world in which we live. When women believe that the only thing important is their happiness, it leads moms to forsake their children and live only for themselves. God help us!

Getting back to the two sides of motherhood, on which side of the coin is your face? Are you overdoing it or under-doing it? I say let's give the coin to Christ and let Him help us find a balance. Just one example of the kind of stability needed as a mom is found in juggling the amount of time we give to our kids' activities. A good guideline is:

## GIVE TIME, BUT DON'T GIVE IN!

While it is true that children spell the word "love," T-I-M-E, there were times, when Nathan and Heidi were younger, that I felt like I was nothing more than a glorified chauffeur. It's so easy to become enslaved to our children's demands and schedules. We somehow think it is what a dedicated mother does and is. There comes a time, however, when we must limit our kids' activities so that we can maintain a home life.

How many of us put a hundred or more miles per day on our vehicles carting our kids around to activities and events that do nothing more than serve to over-saturate their senses? We do so as if it is required to win the "Mommy of the Century" award. As a result, every type of nourishment is sacrificed, from food to family time.

Consider this amazing discovery. Psychologist Blake Bowden at Cincinnati Children's Hospital Medical Center studied 527 adolescents and found that teens who eat dinner at home with their parents at least five times a week are less likely to take drugs, less likely to be depressed, more motivated in their school work, and have a happier social life.

Psychologist Abigail Stewart of the University of Michigan cautioned, however, that simply eating dinner together is not magical. "It's the relationships in the family that count," she said, "and the benefit of eating together simply builds upon that" (USA Today, 8/18/97).

I wonder how much federal funding was spent to figure out that children, regardless of age, need and desire a loving relationship with their parents. And…how many of our hard earned tax dollars went into finding out what our grandmothers already knew. They were aware that the ills of our culture can be healed at the dinner table. It's a sad day when we have to depend on scientific studies to educate us to the benefits of having dinner together as a family.

I'm not proposing that something in the green beans and cornbread is magical and can fix what's wrong with our kids. I do agree, however, that sitting across from our frazzled family members and civilly spending some time interacting is good medicine for any ill.

Mothers! Its time we take back our families. Let's not allow anything, including our role as chauffeur, to keep the family apart. Though it might be a momentous challenge to get everyone to slow down long enough to share a meal, a few minutes per day at the supper table together might spare us from a lifetime of heartache and trouble. May we be wise women and coordinated mothers who are building houses – not tearing them down with our own hands.

# CHAPTER
## SIX

ACHIEVING AND MAINTAINING

CONTENTMENT IS NO SMALL TASK,

ESPECIALLY IN THIS CULTURE.

# I Want To Be Content!

In a book authored by my husband, Steve, entitled *Outdoor Insights* (Harvest House Publishers), he tells about a friend of ours who went camping one weekend to get away from the rigors of city life. Before leaving town, Mike announced to his wife, "I can't wait until we are on our way to the country!" As they were driving out of the city he said, "I can't wait till we get there." Upon arrival he found himself mumbling under his breath, "Oh! I can't wait till camp is set up."

On and on it went. "I can't wait till the fire is built, till supper is cooked, the dishes are cleaned, till we take a walk!" Finally, a light came on in his tired mind. Mike stopped and took a deep breath. He realized he had been so distracted with looking ahead to the next step that the joy of the journey was lost. The whole purpose for getting away from town was being consumed by anxiety. With that revelation, he intentionally slowed his pace and began to bask in the delight of each small part of the camping experience.

It wasn't until Mike was able to relax and take each stride with a contented attitude that he was able to find the tranquillity the trip was supposed to yield. What a vivid picture this story is of the temptation we all must resist. Achieving and maintaining content-ment is no small task, especially in this culture. Every TV commercial screams at our appetites, every maga-zine article tells us we need, and deserve, MORE! Madison Avenue's job is to convince us that we do not have everything we need. Billboards shout at us from every highway about the food we can have, the carpet, the clothes, and the cars we should own. These endless ads tell us our skin is not smooth enough, our hair is not shiny enough and our thighs are definitely not thin enough. The bombardment on our ears and eyes makes us great consumers. However, does it make us content? Not by a long shot!

If I am serious about achieving and maintaining a sense of contentment in my life, there are certain things I find I should never do. For example, I should never read Southern Living Magazine. To me, it is like "female pornography." I find myself lusting after the things in the pictures even though I'm aware I can't have them. Also, I should avoid furniture stores. The big plate glass window of one of these places is like a "peep show" to me. I see, I want. In order to cultivate contentment, I must be careful about what my mind dwells upon. It is sad to admit it, but I know I can get in a want-more-state-of-mind far more quickly than I should. My flesh will always be in a battle with my spirit. Lust is an insatiable thirst.

With that in mind, I know I have to first confess my weakness to the Lord in this area. If I do so, according to II Corinthians 12:9, His power will be poured into my weakness and my weakness will become a container for His power. He will help me be not only justified, but also satisfied!

There are at least three areas of my life where I need His help. I want to be content with:

WHAT I HAVE,

WHO I AM,

WHAT I DO.

# CHAPTER
# SEVEN

COVETING SOMEONE ELSE'S THINGS,

BE IT THEIR HOUSE, THEIR SPOUSE,

THEIR MAID OR NANNY, THEIR VEHICLE,

OR ANYTHING ELSE THAT BELONGS TO THEM,

DIMINISHES THE VALUE OF WHAT GOD

HAS GIVEN TO US.

# Content With What I Have

Hebrews 13:5 instructs, "Let your life be free from the love of money, *being content with what you have* (italics mine), for He Himself has said, 'I will never desert you, nor will I forsake you.' So that we confidently say, 'The Lord is my Helper, I will not be afraid. What shall man do to me?'"

It is quite natural to assume this verse was meant to comfort us in times of crisis. I've used it to do just that. For example, my family and I boarded a flight out of Albany, New York. It was a twin engine, propeller type. We rolled down the runway and lifted off the ground in a strong cross-wind. At about 1500 feet above the earth, suddenly, one of the engines quit. The plane went completely sideways and we were looking at the concrete through our windows. Without hesitation, I cried out, "I will never leave you, nor will I forsake you!" Obviously, we somehow made it back to the terminal (a terrible name for an airport, don't you think?). There we were greeted by emergency vehicles. To say the least, it was a horrifying experience.

Was I right in using that familiar passage in that instance? I truly believe so. And I've used it in other threatening circumstances such as during the middle of the night when I've heard an unfamiliar sound outside the window.

As comforting as it is to quote that scripture in moments such as I've described, have you ever noticed the actual context in which those well-used words appear? They follow a statement about money! Therefore, I don't believe it is a stretch to suggest that this passage can be rightly used as a cry for contentment, something that is a real challenge to find these days.

I Timothy 6:6-10 says, "Of course, there is great gain in godliness combined with contentment; for we brought nothing into this world, so that we can take nothing out of it; but if we have food and clothing, we will be content with these. But those who want to be rich fall into temptation and are trapped by many senseless and harmful desires that plunge people into ruin and destruction. For the love of money is a root of all kinds of evil, and in their eagerness to be rich some have wandered away from the faith and pierced themselves with many pains." Verse 11 continues, "But flee from these things, you man (or woman) of God; and pursue righteousness, godliness, faith, love, perseverance and gentleness."

After specifically encouraging those with limited resources to keep an eye on what is truly important, verse 17 goes on to warn those who have the opposite situation. "Instruct those who are rich in this present world not to be conceited or to fix their hope on the uncertainty of riches, but on God, who richly supplies us with all things to enjoy."

Apostle Paul speaks pointedly in Philippians 4:11-13 concerning the need to foster an attitude of contentment. After thanking the Christians who were concerned with meeting the practical needs of the Apostle at the church in Philippi, Paul goes on to say, "Not that I speak from want; for I have learned to be content in whatever circumstances I am. I know how to get along with humble means, and I also know how to live in prosperity; in any and every circumstance I have learned the SECRET of being filled and going hungry, both of having abundance and suffering need. **I can do all things through Him who strengthens me.**"

How many times I have quoted the familiar last line of this verse. I've used it in situations that range from facing the challenge of staying on the treadmill at the YMCA for just 5 more minutes to looking for a parking spot at the mall during Christmas shopping season. And I've quoted it when a riding lawn mower backed over my ankle and there was no one around but me to lift it off! (The limp didn't last too long!)

It amazes me how I have applied, "I can do all things through Him who strengthens me," to every area of my life...except in the context in which it was written – calling on Christ to help me accomplish the very difficult challenge of finding and maintaining contentment in my life.

Though it is a very real struggle to keep the joy in
the journey by cherishing each step of the way, I do
remember a time in my years that it wasn't such a battle. Not too long ago I found something that reminded me of a simpler time in my life. I was going
through a box of old papers and came upon a checkbook ledger yellowed by the passage of time. It was a
record of all the checks that Steve and I had written in
1977. It became especially interesting when I saw the
specific dates. The record was from the month that
our first child was born. On the eve of Nathan's birth,
we had exactly $20.57 in our checking account. By
the time we brought him home from the hospital it
was down to $4.45.

Strangely enough though, in regards to our serious-
ly limited resources, I do not recall a feeling of panic.
Either I was delirious from labor pains or something
more precious was the matter. We were so caught up
in the joy of the new life that was about to fill our
arms that our meager state was not an issue. Also, our
debt level was at zero. That was a big plus!

When our parents came to see their new grandson,
neither set of them seemed to be concerned with our
simple surroundings. If they were, they didn't indicate
it. Looking back, however, they surely must have been
aghast at how little we had in terms of possessions.
However, they wisely stood by and celebrated in the
arrival of Nathan without commenting on our pover-

ty. (I only hope Steve and I can be as accommodating to our kids if they get married and enter parenthood with as little to their names. What a gift our parents gave to quietly allow us the satisfaction of learning to trust the Lord to provide our needs.)

As time went on, another child, Heidi, arrived in 1980. By then, we were beginning to grow in our work and our checkbook balance went from two figures to three. WOW! We also discovered that those in the business of credit were more open to our appearances at their establishments. So, we began to accumulate both "stuff" and debt. Before too long, we were average Americans with a duplex full of things and a heart full of stress. And you'd think the anxiety that accompanies too much spending would squelch the lust for more stuff. Instead, it seemed to contribute to it. The years that have passed beyond that yellowed checkbook in 1977 have not been without the skirmishes in my heart that reveal my need to know contentment.

One of those battles took place a few years ago when we were attending a large church in Nashville, TN. In order to get to know each other on a personal basis, the staff scheduled what they called "Supper Clubs."* Four couples were chosen to meet together, once a month, for four months in each others' homes. At the end of the four months we were supposed to be intimate friends. Good plan.

We signed up and the pastor's wife asked if we

would be the first host couple. Everything was going along fine until I got the list of folks in our group. I wasn't familiar with two of the couples. However, the remaining one was familiar to me. I didn't know them personally, but I knew about them. I knew of their beautiful house and the fine cars they drove. I had heard about their lovely, summer home, and the tennis court, and swimming pool in their backyard. I knew they were rich folks.

This situation had turned into quite a problem for me. I was at a loss about what to do. I shared my dilemma with Steve and told him who was coming to our modest, brick home for dinner. I sat him down and made the following announcement: "Steve, we have no other choice. We're just gonna to have to move! That's all there is to it. I just can not bring those rich people into our little brick house!"

Where we lived was not the only problem. I was also faced with the terrible question of what I was going to use for dishes. You see, when Steve and I married, we were Hippies. You must understand, Hippies didn't register. Consequently, I didn't receive fine china and crystal for wedding gifts. Unlike rich people, we ate on plain old dishes. Oh! What a terrible mess I was in!

Steve was not sympathetic at all. He thought I was down right silly for being so upset about our house and furnishings. Seeing that I was not going to get any help from Steve, I started doing what any sensible, All-

American woman would do. I went straightway and began cleaning out my underwear drawer, (as though our guests might paw through our personal items). I also went out and bought a new pair of kitchen curtains because one of my children had drawn a picture with a felt-tip pen on the bottom of one of my priscillas.

A few days before the scheduled arrival of "those" guests, I was coming home from taking the kids to school. As I drove along, I was crying out to the Lord about my problem. I poured out my heart concerning my feelings of inferiority and low self-esteem.

He didn't console me with the psycho-babble of our time. He didn't tell me, for example, that it was my mother's absence from my grade school Christmas play that scarred me and caused me to feel so insecure and victimized. Instead, He whispered something in my heart that started a terrible uproar in my spirit. He said, "Annie, you are coveting!" I was breaking one of the top ten! "Thou shalt not covet."

Believe it or not, I had the nerve to argue with God. I told the Lord, "I really don't want their house. I just want one exactly like it. They can keep their stuff. It's O.K. with me. I really don't want theirs, I just want better stuff than I have." I was being sincere with God, but my honesty reeked of arrogance and pride.

Why is coveting so bad? It's not like the other nine commandments. It's not the same as lying about someone and irreparably hurting their reputation. It's not like stealing someone's belongings and leaving them without. It's certainly not murder or adultery. *What could be so wrong about just wanting someone else's stuff?*

Coveting someone else's things, be it their house, their spouse, their maid or nanny, their vehicle, or anything that belongs to them, diminishes the value of what God has given to us. The root sin of covetousness is an *ungrateful heart toward God.*

Most of us are familiar with the account of David and Bathsheba's affair, resulting in David having Bathsheba's husband murdered. However, the underlying problem was something even more sinister than adultery and murder.

The prophet, Nathan, by instruction from the Lord, came to David and told him a story. He told about two men who lived in a certain city. One was a rich man who had a great many flocks and herds. The other man was a poor man who had nothing except one young ewe lamb. The poor man loved his little lamb and he took great care to nourish and care for her. His children played with it. She ate his bread and drank from his cup and even slept on his bosom. She was like a daughter to him.

Now, the rich man was entertaining a traveler. When it came time to prepare the meal, the wealthy host was unwilling to take a lamb from his flock, but rather took the poor man's pet lamb and prepared it for the one who had come to visit.

David was furious. He declared that the rich man deserved to die "because he did this thing and had no compassion."

It was at this point that the prophet Nathan pointed out the truth. He said to David, "You are the man!" David had coveted Uriah's wife, because he didn't think he had enough. Notice what the Lord said to David through Nathan. "The Lord said, 'I made you King of Israel and saved you from the power of Saul. I gave you his palace and his wives and the kingdom of Israel and Judah; and if that had not been enough, I would have given you much more. Why then have you...done this horrible deed?'" (II Samuel 12:7-9)

The terrible act of murdering Uriah was rooted in the sin of covetousness. David had been blessed of God in so many ways, yet he wanted more. In fact, he wanted what God had given to another. Sadly, the story goes on to reveal that this sin led to more deadly transgressions.

God was more than willing to supply not only David's needs, but more abundantly, the desires of his heart. But David's greed displeased the Lord. Like our heavenly Father, most parents would concede that ingratitude in a child is a grievous sin. Unthankful, greedy, and demanding children are a curse to all those around them. Whatever they have never seems to be enough.

Have you ever taken your children for a special day of fun? Perhaps you took them to a very expensive

amusement park. All day long you obeyed their every
whim. You bought them ice cream, soda pop and all
manner of junk food. You rode the rides they wanted
to ride, when they wanted to ride them. Finally, after
spending the day catering to their every desire, you left
the park. On the way home you passed a McDonald's.
Suddenly, all they had experienced through the day
evaporated and they begged you to stop. You responded with a firm, "No, we have to get home." That is
when they pitched a fit as they cried untruthfully,
"You never do anything I want to do." How did it
make you feel when you realized that no matter what
you had given, it was not enough? The disgust you felt
must be similar to that which God feels when His
children are ungrateful for all He has done for them.

Proverbs 30:7-9 says, "Two things I ask of Thee, do
not refuse me before I die: Keep deception and lies far
from me, give me neither poverty nor riches; feed me
with the food that is my portion, lest I be full and
deny Thee and say, 'Who is the Lord?' Or lest I be in
want and steal, and profane the name of my God."

Looking back to my errant attitude regarding the
invasion of the rich folks, it was tempting to blame my
sin on low self-esteem. But I had to honestly ask
myself, "Is that the real problem?" The answer was a
resounding, "NO!" It wasn't that I was thinking less of
myself. Actually, self was all I was thinking about. All
that concerned me was how I would appear in the eyes
of our wealthy visitors.

I would submit that the modern day ill affecting many women is not a lack of self-esteem. Instead, as it was in my case, it is **an obsession with self.** Did low self-esteem contribute to Adam and Eve's downfall in the Garden Of Eden? Absolutely not! To the contrary, it was their preoccupation with their own desires and choosing to please themselves rather than obeying God that brought about their demise. In the same way, men and women currently suffer from too high a self-esteem. Self was the original problem and it still is.

One clear and sad example of this truth is found in the infamous Monica Lewinsky. In her book about her affair with President William J. Clinton, she presented as her reason for her moral failure a low self-esteem. I beg to differ. The evidence proves that she thought higher of herself than the very office of the President, his wife and child, the code of the Seventh Commandment, as well as the welfare of the entire nation. (Unfortunately, the same thing can be said of the President.) It is obvious that Miss Lewinsky had many problems, but low self-esteem was indeed not one of them.

I further submit that to cure the social and spiritual ills in our land, instead of esteeming self, we as women (and men, too), need to cultivate Christ-esteem in our hearts. Only when we look up to Him will we avoid looking down at the vanities of the flesh. Christ said, "...And I, if I be lifted up from the earth, will draw all men unto me." Notice that He didn't say,

"If you will just lift yourself up you'd feel better."
According to Psalm 139, human beings are creations
of great worth and deserve self-*respect*. However, self-
esteem has always been fruitless. It was so in the
Garden of Eden, and it is still true today!

I am fearful of our apparent emphasis these days on
self. It is a dangerous distraction to our quest for
knowing contentment. When I turn on the afternoon
talk shows, I am often appalled at the constant and
consistent message, directed primarily to women, to
*follow the heart.* It is fully designed to bolster "self."
On the surface it sounds appealing and innocent. But
let me sound the warning bells!! If you follow the natural desires of the heart that only serve to elevate the
flesh, you will come to no good end.

Consider the strong admonition God offers in
Jeremiah 17. He warns us to beware of the deception
of putting our trust in our humanness. "Cursed is the
man (or woman) who trusts in mankind and makes
flesh his strength and whose heart turns away from the
Lord" (verse 5). The text goes on to tell the terrible
consequence of trusting in our own hearts and our
own ways. Jeremiah 17:9,10 are very familiar verses
that can save us from falling into this erroneous path
of deception. "The heart is more deceitful than all else
and is desperately sick; Who can understand it? I, the
Lord, search the heart, I test the mind, even to give to
each man according to his ways, according to the
results of his deeds."

God's Word is clear. We cannot trust in our own wisdom and expect to find the motivation to do what is right toward those around us. Our hearts will deceive us to believe that self is to be served first. All others will have to get in line or step aside. There are times, for example, when we may not FEEL like loving our families. We may not FEEL like cooking dinner. We may not FEEL like meeting the sexual needs of a spouse. But we cannot always trust our feelings to lead us to godly actions. If we do, our reward will be lost in the wilderness of self-esteem.

II Chronicles 16:9a says, "For the eyes of the Lord run to and fro throughout the whole earth to show Himself strong on behalf of those whose heart is loyal to Him." Notice that the end of the passage did not say, "loyal to self." Without an undying devotion to walk in His ways, contentment will never be known.

By the way, our "rich folks" showed up at the supper club and they were incredibly friendly. They didn't even go to my chest of drawers and rummage through my underwear. When it was their turn to host an evening, I found it to be most interesting that they used paper plates for the dinner. As it turned out, I had been the snob; they were the gracious ones. We became close friends and still are to this day. And I am far richer in spirit for having gotten to know them.

# CHAPTER
# EIGHT

THE OVER EMPHASIS ON OUTWARD

BEAUTY IS A DECEPTIVE PLAN

OF THE ENEMY OF OUR SOULS,

TO KEEP OUR EYES OFF OF WHAT

WE SHOULD BE WORKING ON.

# Content With Who I Am

Though being satisfied with what I have is a formidable task for me, the second area of my life where I need contentment is even a greater challenge. I want to be content with who I am.

One day, a few years ago, I was watching a TV show that featured an interview with Cheryl Ladd. You may remember that she was one of the later "Charlie's Angels" from the popular series of the late 1970's. The host was obviously enchanted by her and in the course of the interview he posed the question, "If you could change anything about yourself, what would it be?" By the look on the man's face, and the drool that was dripping from his chin, he didn't think there could possibly be anything Ms. Ladd needed to alter to improve her good looks.

As I recall, she looked surprisingly self-conscious and replied, "Well, I think it's quite obvious what I would change." The statement piqued my curiosity to say the least. She looked perfect to me. He asked her to explain. "Of course, I would change my nose." She went on to point out how her nose had an unsightly lump on the side of it, and she could only be photographed from a certain angle in order to hide her imperfection. Well, before they could go to a commercial, I got up out of my chair and went over to the TV set. I moved in really close to the screen to search for this glaring flaw. YEP! There it was! I saw it! There was a tiny little bump on the side of her nose. I'm sure through the years she has had that imperfection surgically remedied, but for the longest time, whenever I saw her, I immediately started looking for the bump. The fact was, she seemed to be absolutely beautiful to the rest of the world, but to her, she saw a bump on her nose. I concluded that no matter what a person looks like, it is nearly impossible to find contentment with our appearance.

As a side note, here's a little free advice, ladies. Stop pointing out your faults to your spouse. Don't say things like, "Just look at these ugly varicose veins. Can you believe how broad my rear-end really is? Just look at all these wrinkles. I look terrible. See how my thighs flap in the wind when I run." Don't do it. If you keep pointing out your flaws and faults, pretty soon he'll start looking at them, the way I looked at Cheryl Ladd, and eventually that's all he'll see. Girls! Men are gullible! If you tell him that you're incredible, he'll believe you!

How sad that our young daughters look at the magazine covers and the teen periodicals and go away feeling inferior. None of us can compete with those computer enhanced, glossy, retouched pictures that are crammed down our throats. If we, as grown adult

women, can't withstand the relentless propaganda
telling us how we are to look, how do we expect our
young daughters, who are more impressionable than
we, to overcome the unattainable standards of the
advertising media? How foolish it is that we would
allow ourselves to be obsessively focused on our
appearance.

There is no denying the overwhelming desire we
have as women to appear attractive. However, the over
emphasis on outward beauty is a deceptive plan of the
enemy of our souls, to keep our eyes off of what we
should be working on. I Peter 3:3,4 tells us that our
beauty "should not come from outward adornment,
such as braided hair and the wearing of gold jewelry
and fine clothes. Instead, it should be that of your
inner self, the unfading beauty of a gentle and quiet
spirit, which is of great worth in God's sight."

Proverbs 31:30 reminds us that "Charm is deceptive, and beauty is fleeting; but a woman who fears the
Lord is to be praised." Once again I am faced with just
how upside down this world is. God is telling us to
work on our "inward looks" while the world is always
pushing the outward appearance.

In Barbara Dafoe Whitehead's book, *The Girls of
Gen X,* she writes, "The number one wish among
young women, outranking the desire to end home-
lessness, poverty, or racism is to get and stay thin."

Battling the pounds is a "weighty" issue in my life.
In my adult years I have weighed sixty pounds more

than I do, and twenty pounds less than I presently am. It has taken a long time to come to grips with this ongoing struggle, that my worth is more than what the scales say. Every time I buy panty hose, and check the graph on the back of the package to make sure I'm buying the correct size for my present weight, I am reminded that the world stands in judgment of my success or failure to control my weight. We live in an unforgiving culture when it comes to our appearance. If we are going to achieve a sense of contentment with who we are, we are going to have to fight for it.

Steve's mother, Lillian, was a raving beauty in her younger days. Of course, she is a lovely lady today in her early 70's. But in her "hay day" she had the measurements of the Ford Models, 36-22-34. She told me about the day she was looking in the mirror and assessing what time had done to her. She said that she looked at the wrinkles and the added pounds and concluded, "I am fearfully and wonderfully made." That is the truth.

There is a woman in the scriptures who struggled with being content with her body. If anyone had a right to feel badly, it was this woman. "And the woman who had a hemorrhage for twelve years, and had endured much at the hands of many physicians, and had spent all that she had was not helped at all, but rather had grown worse, after hearing about Jesus came up in the crowd behind Him and touched His cloak. For she thought, 'If I just touch His garments,

I shall get well.' And immediately the flow of her blood was dried up; and she felt in her body that she was healed of her affliction. And immediately Jesus, perceiving in Himself that the power proceeding from Him had gone forth, turned around in the crowd and said, 'Who touched my garments?'...But the woman fearing and trembling, aware of what had happened to her, came and fell down before Him, and told Him the whole truth." Verse 34, "And he said to her, 'Daughter, your faith has made you well; go in peace, and be healed of your affliction'"(Mark 5:25-34).

This woman had created a real problem for herself by violating a Levitical law.** The Jews had stringent hygiene standards regarding their dealings with blood. (That's why Kosher meat has to be prepared in such a way that all the blood from the animal is drained. The meat has to be either smoked or salted.) Because of her hemorrhaging, the law demanded that the woman be declared "unclean." Wherever she sat was "unclean," whoever she touched was declared "unclean." I'm convinced that she looked horrible and smelled even worse. After twelve years of this scourge, she was known and labeled as a person to avoid. She knew if she dared to touch Jesus, she faced the risk of being found out. Still, believing that Jesus could make the difference, she reached out to touch Him. And sure enough, the truth was made known.

I love the part of this story where she came to Jesus and told him the "whole" truth. I can only imagine what a flood of emotion that flowed from her heart. After twelve long years of torturous despair, she had finally found the Healer. She told him how she had spent everything she had and was NOT HELPED AT ALL. She was even worse than when she started.

Like all the others who had called her "unclean" and turned her away, Jesus could have done the same. Instead, Jesus looked at her with compassion, even after she told Him the "whole" truth, and He called her DAUGHTER! That, my friend, is the good news! No matter what you've done, no matter what others have said about you, go to Jesus, tell Him the "whole" truth and He will accept you and call you DAUGH-TER.

You may say in response, "But you don't know what I've done. The fact is, I had an abortion." Or, "I was the 'easy' girl in school." You might confess, "I've been unfaithful to my husband." Still worse, "I've abused my children." "I have disgraced my parents." On and on the possibilities go and the facts are stacked against you.

With my thanks to the writer, Charles Bates, for the following incredible insight, let me offer some good news that is graced with hope. We serve a God who is far more interested in the **truth** than He is in the **facts.**

While these two factors may seem similar, they are quite opposed to each other when it comes to the way God sees things. Consider this:

FACT: Moses killed the Egyptian.

TRUTH: God wanted to use Moses to free His people.

FACT: David was responsible for the murder of Uriah.

TRUTH: David was the apple of God's eye.

FACT: Sarah was too old to have a baby.

TRUTH: God had called her to be the mother of nations.

FACT: The Widow of Nain, weeping because of her deceased son, was leaving the city of Jerusalem with him in the coffin.

TRUTH: Jesus was coming into the city and He was going to give the widow back her son. She thought she knew the facts, but the truth was approaching her on the road. That "truth" was Jesus.

From these examples, it is evident that God is more interested in the truth than He is in the *facts!*

I have seen first hand the vast contrast between the facts and the truth. One day I was shopping with my mother. At the time, she was suffering from cancer and her body had become her worst enemy. Her body was killing her. We were trying to find her a dress for a family wedding and we had to go into the maternity clothes section to find something that would accommodate her swollen belly. As we stood in the dressing room, mom in her bra and panties, with her cancerous stomach protruding, she said, "I never thought I'd ever have such an ugly body." Her statement caught me totally off guard, because I had never seen anyone so beautiful.

If I were to ask the health officials whether my mother had value, they would have given me the facts. She had outlived her usefulness. She was a drain on the health dollars for her age group. She was terminally ill and would not recover. Those were the facts. But the truth was, she had value beyond compare. She was not loved because she was valuable, she was valuable because she was loved. In March of 1996 we said farewell to her. Two and half years later, weakened by grief and a disease of the heart, my father passed away.

After they both died, the six children met to divide up the household furniture and other personal items. My baby sister wanted mom and dad's bedroom suite. The room in which it was located was rather damp. Consequently, the finish was gone. Also, one of the legs had been broken. Still, my sister took the suite to a man to have it refinished and repaired. He took one look at the furniture and told her it would take at least $2000 to have it refinished. He then offered his opinion of the value of the furniture. He said, "If it were me, I'd sell this junk for a couple of hundred dollars and get some real furniture. Look, it's just Montgomery Ward and it has no value."

As she stood across the counter from the man, my sister fought hard to hold back the tears. She told him, "Sir, I didn't want the furniture because I thought it was worth money. I wanted it because it belonged to my mom and dad." Her response silenced the insensitive man.

One of my favorite TV shows is "The Antique Roadshow" on PBS. It's hard to imagine, but one episode they featured a lady who bought a table for just under $30 at a garage sale and then sold it for nearly $500,000 at a well known New York City auction. Anyway, whenever I watch this show I am amazed at the value of some of the items. A lamp or picture can look unimpressive, even be unattractive, but when they find the name of the creator marked on the item, the value goes up considerably. One minute it's just a plain old chair or lamp or vase. The next minute it is a treasure of great value, because of the one who made it.

How many of us have been standing on the auction block of life and those around us have declared our lack of value? Perhaps as a child you heard the words that still ring in your ears, "worthless," "no good," "stupid," "immoral," "dumb." Perhaps you look at your body and, like the woman with the issue of blood, you are saying of yourself, "Unclean!" Your breast may be gone and your body holds the marks of the surgeon's scalpel. Yet it's time you agreed with God. You are "fearfully and wonderfully made." You have worth...because God made you. Your value is not dependent on your pedigree, your educational degrees, nor your appearance. It is because you belong to God that you have been called "Daughter!" That, my friend, is good news.

One more example of how truth outweighs the facts is found in one of my dearest friends. She is truly a remarkable woman. She has several children and home schools them all. She is a wonderful homemaker. She sews, cooks, and is possibly the most thoughtful person alive. And, what's really sickening, she doesn't even scream at her children. Can you imagine that?

One day she told me something I will never forget. She confided that each time she gave birth to one of her sweet little babies, and they laid the child in her arms, the first thing that came to her mind was, "Someday, this child will learn to count, and then they will figure out that I was pregnant when I got married." Oh, how sad. She had been caught in the quicksand of looking at the facts, instead of dwelling on the truth. The facts will always stack against us. Only the truth will set us free. The truth is, my friend is a lovely, redeemed daughter of God.

Why do we let ourselves believe the facts are more important than the truth? Some of us get up in the mornings and we despise our bodies because we carry around a few extra pounds. We see wrinkles and gray hair and we think we have no value. Shame on us all. God has told us the truth...we are cherished in His

sight. How do we know? "But God demonstrated His love toward us, in that while we were yet sinners, Christ died for us"
(Romans 5:8).

# CHAPTER
## NINE

HARDLY ANY CONFLICT IS UGLIER

THAN THE WAR BETWEEN WOMEN WHO

WORK INSIDE THE HOME AND THOSE

WHO WORK OUTSIDE THE HOME.

# Content With What I Do

There is nothing sadder than a civil war. When family and friends fight, it's more vicious and more bloody than when strangers go at it. But when Christian women take "pot shots" at each other, it's more than sad, it's a sin.

Hardly any conflict is uglier than the war between women who work inside the home and those who work outside the home. Some of the nastiest accusations are made on this battleground. As I stated earlier, a mother who has a little baby is making a terrible, tragic mistake if she elects to hire someone to raise her baby. Simply stated, I don't think you can pay someone to love your child. And children need love just as much as they need their diapers changed. All kinds of studies have been done in orphanages where they find that babies who are not held, talked to and shown love do not thrive and sometimes do not even survive. No matter how much money the government wants to pay child care providers, they cannot pay someone to be "Mommy."

Now that you know where I stand, let me say it is completely unnecessary for the hateful attitudes that are sometimes displayed between Christian women when it comes to the decision of whether to work inside or outside of the home.

I have heard women who work outside the home refer to women who work inside the home as lazy, lacking ambition, and worse. The statement that women who work inside the home do nothing but lie around all the time and eat bon bons is inaccurate and mean spirited.

Comments like these are hurtful and unfair, but so are some other comments I've heard said about women who work outside the home. I've heard ladies who work at home say that those who work outside are "money hungry," that they don't love their children, and that they only care about having bigger and better stuff.

The judgmental attitudes on both sides are wrong. In Luke 10 we read about two sisters, Mary and Martha, who both loved Jesus and enjoyed His company. We read about the day when Jesus came to visit these sisters and their brother. "Now as they were traveling along, He entered a certain village; and a woman named Martha welcomed Him into her home. And she had a sister called Mary, who moreover was listening to the Lord's word, seated at His feet. But Martha was distracted with all her preparations; and she came up to Him, and said, 'Lord, do You not care that my sister has left me to do all the serving alone? Then tell her to help me.' But the Lord answered and said to her, 'Martha, Martha, you are worried and bothered about so many things; but only a few things are necessary, really only one, for Mary has chosen the good part, which shall not be taken away from her.'"

I don't believe this rebuke would have been handed out to Martha had she not brought her opinion of what Mary should be doing into the conversation. First, she was assuming that Mary was going to help her, although she had nothing to do with the plans Martha had made. Secondly, Martha took Mary's lack of participation much too personally by accusing Jesus of being unfeeling ("Don't you care that my sister has left me to do all the work?").

Martha thought Mary should have the same calling as she did. When we start to assume that we know what everyone else should be doing and start telling them what to do, that's when we step over the line. What Mary was doing was indeed important. But what Martha was doing was equally significant.

We need to do what we are supposed to do, and let others be obedient to the Lord. My work, for example, may be completely different than yours. The choices I had to make were unique to my situation. The best way to describe it is to tell about the day Heidi and I were watching one of the talk shows that featured an argument about whether women should work inside or outside the home. She turned to me and asked, "Mom, were you a stay-at-home mom?" I replied, "No, Heidi, you were a take-along-kid!" Looking back, I'm convinced it was the right choice for our family.

At this moment, in light of Mary and Martha's conflict, you may be reassessing your vocation. Perhaps
you feel that some changes may be necessary.
Admittedly, it is an enormously difficult decision that
we women have to make regarding our work. Some
families think the mother has to take a job outside the
home regardless of what is best for the children
because of the financial commitments they have
made. I challenge you, as a couple, to sit down together and evaluate the honest condition of your finances.
If you are working outside the home and are reluctantly forfeiting your time with your children, you
may suffer from a self-loathing that is stealing your
contentment. Perhaps you and your spouse need to
develop a long term plan such as the one set out in
Larry Burkette's book, *Women Leaving The Workplace*
(Moody Press). He offers some practical advice on
how to make the needed changes in a timely fashion
without collapsing the family finances.

However, if you have entered, or plan to enter, a
workplace outside the home, be very careful not to
allow yourself to be deceived. Let me remind you once
again of Jeremiah 17:9: "The heart is deceitful above
all things, and desperately wicked: who can know it?"
If a lack of contentment with what you have and who
you are is the thing that is driving you away from
home just so you can get more and better stuff and
feel better about yourself, then you will never be con-

tent with what you do. May God guide you. And as He does, may He help you live by the wisdom found in Proverbs 10:9 and Colossians 3:23-24.

"Whatsoever thy hand findeth to do, do it with thy might..."

"And whatsoever ye do, do it heartily, as to the Lord, and not unto men; knowing that of the Lord ye shall receive the reward of the inheritance: for ye serve the Lord Christ." (KJV)

# CHAPTER
## TEN

I WAS DESPERATE FOR RELIEF...

I WAS WILLING TO DO WHAT

THE COUNSELOR TOLD ME TO DO.

I WAS SICK AND TIRED OF BEING

SICK AND TIRED.

# Courageous

It is difficult to be courageous in a day when you fear for the survival of decency. The moral decay of this nation and its leaders tempts one to doubt the certainty of the future for you and me, our children, and our grandchildren. I think it is safe to say that all of us long for the joy and security of a bright tomorrow.

The virtuous woman of Proverbs 31 somehow managed to cultivate an attitude that I want for my life. In verse 25, the passage says of this woman, "Strength and dignity are her clothing, and *she smiles at the future*" (italics mine).

Oh! How I long to look ahead with hope. However, smiling at the future not only seems scary at times, but utterly impossible. Maybe you are facing a future filled with questions concerning your health or financial survival. Perhaps your marriage is on shaky ground, your child is rebellious, or your insane and obnoxious in-laws are coming to live with you. If any of these things, or something as traumatic, is staring at you like a hungry wolf, then you know very well that smiling at the future will require not only great courage, but also an absolute miracle.

How can it be done? How can we possibly look

down the road of life with a "glory grin" when everything around begs us to throw up our hands and say,
"Woe is me!" How can we avoid being frightened fol-
lowers of Christ and instead, be courageous Christians
marching on with our heads up? In my own experience, in order to bravely face the future, I discovered
there was one particular challenge that helped me
more than anything else. It was when I was willing to:

## Confront the Past

It is painful to recount it, but there was an unspeak-
able thing that occurred in my early years that caused
me to be a terribly unhappy child. Yet, it was this
dreadful situation and the ongoing repercussions that
God used to accomplish a mighty work in my life.
But...it wasn't until I was willing to confront the
truth and deal with the residue from the past that I
was able to find the courage to let go of it and go on
with God.

In the story of Joseph, beginning in Genesis 37, I
find a source of comfort. Though his circumstances
may have been different, I somehow relate to the path
he walked from victimized to victorious. As the
youngest of twelve and the favored son of Jacob,
Joseph experienced great betrayal and damage from
his brothers who had a deadly case of sibling rivalry
toward him. One day, the seventeen year old went out,

by request of his father, to basically spy on his brothers to see if they were doing their work correctly. The brothers decided they had had enough of the young "troublemaker" and their disdain for him boiled in their hearts.

You probably already know the story of how Jacob loved Joseph and showed favoritism toward him by giving him the famous coat of many colors. When his brothers saw Joseph coming, wearing "that" coat, they decided to get rid of him once and for all.

The brothers stripped the young man of his richly ornamented robe and threw him into a dry pit. Then, without remorse, they sat down to eat their lunch. As they munched, they contemplated what they should do with such an irritating nuisance. They talked about killing him, but fortunately for Joseph, greed won over malice and they decided to sell him into slavery for twenty shekels of silver (equivalent to $12.80).

The pit into which Joseph was thrown was actually a dry cistern. The mouth of it was smaller at the top than the bottom, so it was virtually impossible for Joseph to get out of the pit on his own.

Joseph was eventually sold to the Ishmaelites who, then took him to Egypt and sold him to Potiphar, Pharaoh's officer, the captain of the bodyguard.

When Joseph was sold as a slave, he lost everything. He was deprived of his inheritance, his family, his language, his religion, his wealth, and the love and affection of his father. He was placed in a heathen home,

in a pagan culture, far away from the rich Jewish life
to which he was accustomed.

Genesis 39:2 says, "And the Lord was with Joseph,
so he became a successful man. And he was in the
house of his master, the Egyptian. Now his master saw
that **the Lord was with him** and how the Lord caused
all that he did to prosper in his hand. So Joseph found
favor in his sight, and became his personal servant;
and he made him overseer over his house, and all that
he owned he put in his charge." What an amazing
turn of events for someone who had once been in a
pitiful pit! But…the story doesn't end there!

As you may recall, Potiphar was not the only one
who was impressed with Joseph. Genesis 39:6 says
that Joseph was handsome in form and appearance.
Enter Potiphar's wife! She began to pursue the young,
handsome servant. However, Joseph refused her
advances. It would seem that if anyone had an excuse
for looking for love and affection anywhere it was
made available, it would have been Joseph. Robbed of
all that was rightfully his, the loneliness must have
been terrible. Yet, he replied in verse 9 of chapter 39,
"How then could I do this great evil, and sin against
God?"

Day after day, the scheming wife of the absent
Potiphar pursued Joseph, begging him to lie with her.
He continued to resist her seduction. One day in
order to avoid her sexual advances, he ran from her,
leaving his garment in her hand. Humiliated by her

lack of success with Joseph, she decided to seek revenge for his lack of compliance. In her apparent rage, she falsely accused him of attempted rape. His garment in her hands became the evidence of his assault.

Joseph was consequently sent to prison. He was jailed not for doing wrong, but for doing right! The passage reads, however, "But **the Lord was with Joseph** and extended kindness to him, and gave him favor in the sight of the chief jailer," and, "**...the Lord was with him;** and whatever he did, the Lord made to prosper" (verses 21 and 23).

As the account continues, the recurring phrase throughout is "the Lord was with him." Even when Joseph suffered wrongly and was put in a terrible situation, God was with him. To be honest, I've never been comfortable with this part of the story. I don't want God to be with me in the midst of trouble, I want Him to deliver me out of the trouble...especially if I feel that I don't deserve to suffer. However, life is not always filled with "Little House On The Prairie" endings. Many of us are called to suffer, even when we are not the one who has sinned.

At this moment, you may be saying in protest, "Hey! Wait just a minute Miss Annie! Are you saying that the 'pit' or the 'jail' I'm in is where God has led me?" My response is a respectful, "Yes!"

And you may retort, "I want out! Why would God do this to me?" May I say as gently as it can be written, "My friend, it is in the 'pit' or in the 'prison' that one is most challenged with the core belief that...**no matter what happens, God will take care of me.** Let's look ahead at this story about Jacob's blessed son. What happened to him will reveal the answer to the cry of your heart.

Joseph was first thrown into a **pit,** then cruelly sold as a slave to Potiphar. Then, for something he didn't do, he was condemned to **prison.** But...God's ultimate destination for him was the **palace,** where he would be used in an incredible way to save his own people.

At this point in the story of Joseph's journey, it is extremely critical that careful notice be given to his response to the evil that had been done to him. It must be understood that the outcome might have been totally different if Joseph had chosen to become bitter and wallow in the mud of despair. It is our response to the trouble that determines whether we experience success or failure.

Instead of resenting the path he had been forced to walk, Joseph chose to see God's all-powerful hand in his life. He accepted even the unjust suffering as coming from God. As you may recall, the famine that struck Egypt caused the surrounding peoples to seek help. Joseph's family was not exempt from the desperate need. Jacob sent his other sons to appeal for the staples that would ensure their survival. As a result, when the sons of Jacob went before the one who was

in authority over the goods that were being distrib-
uted, they had an unexpected, yet overdue, encounter.
Genesis 45 records the moment when Joseph con-
fronted his evil brothers. "Then Joseph could not control himself before all those who stood by him, and he
cried, 'Have everyone go out from me.' So there was
no man with him when Joseph made himself known
to his  brothers. And he wept so loudly that the
Egyptians heard it, and the household of Pharaoh
heard of it."

"Then Joseph said to his brothers, 'Please come
closer to me.' And they came closer. And he said, 'I am
your brother Joseph, whom you sold into Egypt. And
now do not be grieved or angry with yourselves,
because you sold me here; for God sent me before you
to preserve life.'"

"...Now, therefore, it was not you who sent me
here, but God; and He has made me lord of all Egypt"
(verses 1-8). I once read a translation that put it this
way, "What man meant for evil, God worked for
good."

Joseph forgave those who had despitefully used and
abused him. It is quite evident that his heart was filled
with forgiveness instead of bitterness because of the
names he gave to his children. He named his first born
son Manasseh, which means, "God has made me forget all my troubles and all my father's household." He
then named his second son Ephraim, which means,
"God has made me fruitful in the land of my affliction."

Joseph's triumph is a demonstration that God can make good out of any bad that comes into a life. If you will be courageous enough to confront the past then you will come to see how all "your steps have been ordered" by Him (Psalm 37:23 and Romans 8:28). With the foundation of trust in His mighty ability to lead you, then, like Joseph, you can turn to face the intense challenge that often accompanies an honest confrontation with the past—forgiving those who have wronged or hurt you.

What happens when you choose not to forgive and instead cling foolishly to the hurts? The following lyric not only shows the result of unforgiveness, but it also directs you to the "key" that will unlock an important, life changing door for you.

## THE KEY

I cannot tell you how I was hurt
But I'll tell you I've had some tears
I cannot tell you who it was
That turned my trust into fears
So I took the pieces of my broken heart
I built some prison walls
And there I've held that offender for years
And this is what I thought
"He'll never know freedom
As long as I live
I'll never give him freedom."

Then one day the Visitor came
To this prison in my heart
He said, "You ought to know the truth about
The one behind the bars
Yes, he's weak and he's weary
He has not smiled in years
And you have been successful
At keeping his eyes filled with tears
But Oh! How he longs for his freedom
These words are the key
They first came from me
'Father forgive them'
Come let me show you how to use them."

He said, "Don't you know the offender
Is rarely the one in pain
Instead, the one who will not forgive
Is the one who wears the chains."
So I opened up the prison door
I used forgiveness as the key
And when I let that prisoner go
I found that it was Me!
Oh! How sweet is the freedom
It came on the day
When my heart could say
"Father, forgive them!"
"Father, forgive them!"

(Steve Chapman/Times & Seasons Music/BMI)

Perhaps you realize at this moment that you are the one behind the bars. Could it be that you desperately desire to know the joy that follows the opening of the prison door with the key of forgiveness?

Perhaps you have tried to forgive. You've prayed and cried aloud, "I FORGIVE!"...only to be disappointed when the "bad" feelings returned...and you're wondering if it really worked. If that is true for you, perhaps my own experience with facing the "pit" of my past, and those who put me there, will offer some assistance.

In order to help you with the process of forgiveness, it is very important to first remind you that it is the only choice that will lead to a healthy life—physically, emotionally, and spiritually. Psalm 31:10 reveals that our bones are "consumed" by iniquity. An unforgiving heart is one that harbors sin. The Lord's prayer, as recorded in Matthew 6, instructs us to "forgive our debtors" in order to be forgiven. Until we make the choice to extend that divine courtesy to others, we hold onto iniquity. The result is...the very bones that help support the body begin to waste away. It is as though spiritual sickness causes physical illnesses.

Another lyric based on a true story might serve to illustrate the damaging effect that bitterness and unforgiveness can have on a life.

## TWO CHILDREN

Two children
A brother and a sister
Born to a father
Who was a slave to wine
They do remember
Their younger years of sorrow
How their daddy used to hurt them
Time after time

But somehow they grew to be so different
They both turned out to be like day and night
One lives in peace
Up in Ohio
One was bitter
'Til the day she died

I wondered, "What could make the difference
In the two of them
Both had reasons to be bitter
But one was so sweet
How could one live in peace
And not the other."
Not long ago the answer
Came clear to me
I saw the brother at his daddy's grave
Placing flowers there
His eyes were filled with tears
He said, "Daddy, once again I do forgive you

For the way you made us suffer through the years."

Now I can see how the two could be so
different
How their lives turned out to be like day and night
He lives in forgiveness up in Ohio
She was bitter 'til the day she died
He lives in peace up in Ohio
She was bitter 'til the day she died
A bitter heart was the reason that she died.

(Steve Chapman/Dawn Treader Music)

I personally know the people about whom this song
was written. On first reading, you may think that the
sister in the story was so abused by the dad that she
could not forgive. And, you might assume that the
brother was able to "live in peace" because he was not
the one as adversely affected by an abusive, alcoholic
father. However, you might be surprised to learn that
indeed it was the brother who was extremely battered
by the dad, even to the point of a lifelong, debilitating
handicap that resulted. The sister was so consumed
with hatred for what was done to her brother that
eventually, her very life was destroyed by bitterness.
Her brother made a choice that yielded peace, she
chose a path of self-destruction. What a sad and need-
less tragedy!

Does the level of bitterness in the sister's heart ring
the proverbial bell in your mind? She experienced

nothing short of the torture that befell the unforgiving servant in Matthew 18.

The story tells of a slave who owed his master ten thousand talents. (This was about 10 million dollars in silver content, but worth much more in buying power.) The slave had no means of payment and so the lord commanded that the slave and all his family be sold and repayment be made. The slave fell down, prostrated himself before the master, and begged for mercy, declaring that he would repay the debt. Of course, this was absurd. There was no way a slave could pay such a huge debt in the course of his lifetime. Yet the master felt compassion and released the slave, forgiving him the entire debt.

But the slave went out and found a fellow slave who owed him a hundred denari (a denarius was equivalent to one day's wage), seized him, and began to choke him, saying, "Pay back what you owe."

The fellow slave fell down and began to entreat him, saying, "Have patience with me and I will repay you." However, the one who had been forgiven an impossible debt refused to show mercy on a fellow servant who could eventually repay his debt. The unreasonable slave had his fellow servant thrown into prison until he could pay back all that he owed.

The master heard about this and called the unforgiving slave to himself. He said, "You wicked slave, I forgave you all the debt because you entreated me. Should you not also have had mercy on your fellow slave, even as I had mercy on you?" The unforgiving slave was then handed over to the torturers until he could repay all that was owed him. Verse 35 says, "So shall My heavenly Father also do to you, if each of you does not forgive his brother from your heart."

I personally know the hopeless pit and the cruel prison of bitterness. However, I can report that I have also experienced the beautiful palace of forgiveness. But as wonderful as it is, I'll be the first to admit that the process toward that palace is not an easy path.

By the time I was 20 years old, I had been able to compartmentalize my life. I had many days that were fine. I had great friends and I was doing well in school. I loved the Lord as much as I could. However, there were times when I would become totally debilitated. Whenever anyone would make mention of any kind of sexual assault or abuse, I would find myself with my head hanging out the window with dry heaves and hyperventilating. This was a real nuisance, since I felt relatively normal at any other time. It was a close friend who had observed this peculiar behavior in me that took matters into her own hands and made arrangements for me to talk to a counselor about the problem. As much as I balked at this meeting, I realized that the unresolved situation in my past was affecting my everyday life more and more. I didn't want to be an emotional and spiritual cripple, so I agreed to meet with this man.

Up until that time I had never spoken of the "incident" with anyone. When I went home from the courtroom trial as a six year old, no one knew how to help me. Though I am confident that they meant no further harm at the time, my parents thought it would be best if we all just forgot about it. Well…perhaps some forgot, but I certainly didn't and neither did my parents. No one knew how to deal with the pain, and so, we all suffered alone. Nonetheless, I tried to push the thoughts aside and get on with my life.

Talking to the counselor was one of the most difficult things I had ever done up to that time. I literally had to force the words out of my mouth. Telling a stranger was bad enough; telling a man was even worse. My thirty minute appointment turned into two grueling hours. When my visit with him was over, I left and never returned. I have been told since that no one can get over such a scarring situation in only one session. My response to that statement is, "It's according to how badly you want help!" I was desperate for relief; therefore I was willing to do what the counselor told me to do. I was sick and tired of being sick and tired. I was ready to be free from years of bondage and torment.

In my book *Running on Empty (And Looking For The Nearest Exit),* I quoted Neil T. Anderson (Bethany House Publishers). He says in *The Bondage Breakers,* "Forgiveness is costly; we pay the price of the evil we forgive. Yet you're going to live with those consequences whether you want to or not; your only choice

is whether you will do so in the bitterness of unforgiveness or the freedom of forgiveness." I somehow
understood that forgiveness would be emotionally and
physically expensive. After all...it cost Christ his life.
That realization tempted me to run and hide again
under the strangely comforting blanket of suffering
that had been mine for so long. Also, it was not any
consolation at all to realize that forgiveness would cost
me the right to revenge.

After I became a Christian, I became keenly aware
that who and what I was supposed to be as a born
again believer was not who and what I was inside my
heart and mind. I tried to live the Christian life in a
moral, loving way. For the most part I experienced
God's divine reconstruction work in my life. I desperately wanted to be that new creature in Christ with
old things passing away and all things becoming new
(II Cor 5:17). There was great comfort in my heart as
I recognized God's merciful work in my life.
However, there was one area that seemed to hold me
back. I hated the man who had harmed me. I hated
him with a vengeance. So, even though I loved God
and wanted His best for me, I was guilty of violating
the heart of I John 4:20,21. "If someone says, 'I love
God,' and hates his brother, he is a liar; for the one
who does not love his brother whom he has seen, cannot love God whom he has not seen. And this commandment we have from Him, that the one who loves
God should love his brother also."

Realizing that a Christian was supposed to love everyone and hate no one, I knew I had a problem. For a long time I would simply deny my thoughts of hatred toward that man. After talking to the counselor, I was challenged with the re-occurring thought that, "perhaps I should try *being honest* with God." So, whenever a thought of hatred and revenge came to my mind, instead of trying to push it back, I brought it out in the open. This was my first step toward opening the door of the prison I had been in for so long. I would EXPOSE MY THOUGHTS to God in prayer. I would pray something like this: "Dear Lord, You see this vile, wicked thought that I am having. I know You see how much I want this person to die and go to hell. Lord, I give this thought, and all my thoughts, to You and ask You to forgive me and change my heart."

As I learned to be honest with God, I came to a very painful realization. All my life I had looked at the offense from the point of view as a child. My only perspective was one of innocence. I would say, "I was just a little child. I had done nothing wrong."

Of course, I was not responsible, in any way, for this particular sinful act. However, as long as I saw the situation as, "I was the innocent child and he was the monster molester," there was no room for forgiveness. There was too big a chasm between the offender and me. It was only when I could admit that I too was a sinner, in the eyes of God, that I could see myself on the same level, needing the same undeserved grace, as the perpetrator.

So part of my exercise in honesty was recognizing my innate need of forgiveness. In Psalm 51:5 David states, "Behold, I was brought forth in iniquity, and in sin my mother conceived me." The "sin" condition was present, even though I was a child.

Along with **exposing my wicked thoughts,** I would take the second step to freedom. I would TURN MY THOUGHTS TO PRAYERS OF THANKSGIVING. I would pray, "Thank You, Lord for this wicked thought because it has reminded me to pray and seek Your help. Thank You that You are my source of strength and You are not embarrassed by anything I could think or do."

Next, I would QUOTE SCRIPTURES on forgiveness and love, all the while concentrating on those passages to reaffirm the correctness of my prayers. The last part of my prayer was, by far, the most difficult. I would **pray that God would save the offender,** allow him to know God's grace, and take him to heaven. (I eventually discovered that it is very hard to keep hating someone when you are praying for them.)

Many times each day I would go through the same process. I understand the seventy times seven instruction that Jesus gave in Matthew 18:22. Though my emotions were far, far from sincere, I knew I had to discipline myself to follow through...because I was desperate to be free. Forgiveness was my only hope and I worked on it feverishly.

I started on this process to forgiveness out of an act of desperate obedience. Needing to be free from the torment of unforgiveness and anger, I obeyed the instructions of the counselor. I exercised my will to forgive. But, after a time, as my heart softened, my obedience turned from a soulish act of wanting to feel better, to a spiritual desire to honor God. After about six months, I woke up one morning and realized that the chains had fallen away. I was finally free! Was this the last time I had to struggle with this issue? I wish it was, but the same discipline that was needed in the first six months has been needed each time I've faced reminders and dealt with the residue effect of what was done to me. However, I gladly say, it has gotten easier each time I have had to deal with the memories.

Today, I am happy to say, I am not a VICTIM, I am a VICTOR in Jesus Christ. I can thankfully say, "I am no longer living in the pit, or the prison, but in the palace of the King as His child." And if He can help me through that process, I know He can deliver you as well. Whatever lurks "back there," take great courage in knowing that He can be your source of victory over it!

# CHAPTER
# ELEVEN

TRUE COURAGE DOES NOT

MEAN THE ABSENCE OF FEAR,

BUT RATHER PROCEEDING IN

THE FACE OF IT.

# Impact The Present

Courage builds on courage. When we can look back and say as Samuel said after crossing the Jordan River on dry ground, "Thus far the Lord has helped us" (1 Samuel 7:12), it seems to lift our countenance and encourages us to press on. On the foundation of the courage required to confront the past, we can find the strength needed to impact the present.

One day my sister and her husband came to see us. We decided it would be great fun to take a picnic lunch to the local marina. They had terrific picnic facilities and when we were finished eating, the children chased crawdads and caught minnows and the husbands fished. My sister and I sat under a tree and talked. We were having a great time. The afternoon came to an end and we were packing up our belongings and were just about ready to leave. About that time, a couple in a ski boat arrived at the nearby ramp and started putting their boat into the water. It became obvious that the woman was going to do some serious sun bathing. In fact, she decided to begin her tanning process before they left the dock.

She was wearing one of those "thong" swimsuits. Actually, I could say more precisely what she was not

wearing. (A thong swimsuit, for you who are shel-
tered, is a bikini bottom that is basically just a string
up the back-side.) Can you imagine deliberately doing
this to yourself?! I can see this happening by accident.
You may be out shopping and things get a little twist-
ed and you end up with this predicament against your
will. But doing this to yourself on purpose? I don't
think so!

Anyway, this woman positioned herself on top of
the motor cover of the boat. She perched herself in full
view with her rear-end shining in the mid-day sun.
Our children, and we believe our husbands as well,
could see the sight. (Steve and Bill claimed they didn't
see a thing.) Oh, well.

Now, you must understand, my sister has a charac-
ter twist that makes her a lot of fun to be with.
Sometimes, she will say things before she has a chance
to think it through. It was no different that day. We
were all standing in amazement of this indecent spec-
tacle, when my sister, without warning any of us, suddenly yelled something across the water. Keep in mind
that water is a great conductor of sound. So, what
started out a civilized volume ended up with a rather
"megaphone" effect. My sister unreservedly called to
the scantily clad woman in the boat, **"Excuse me,
your butt's in the air."**

For some reason, that hit my funny bone and I
laughed so hard I thought I was going to wet myself.
I looked at her in total shock and proud amazement.

Then she said something to me that has literally changed my life. **"If she has enough nerve to show it, I have enough nerve to tell her I see it."**

As time passed that memorable day at the dock, I thought about all the times I've allowed other peoples' wrong behavior to silence me. Often when we are faced with cultural and moral corruption, we are indeed the "silenced" ones. That day my mind...and my heart...was changed.

The new inspiration that my sister's courage had instilled in me came in handy one day when I was at the local mall. I was walking down the long corridor past the stores when I happened to pass a picture gallery. I took notice of one of the very realistic paintings on display. It was a woman nude from the waist up. As I passed by, I was furious. "How could they have a picture like that in a public mall? Of all the nerve!!"

I started to walk on by, but suddenly, something unusual happened. Across the waters of that lake, down the highway, through the parking lot, through the double doors of that mall, came "those words." They echoed through my mind. Without hesitating, I turned on my heels and said, **"Excuse me, but somebody's butt's in the air!!"** People within ear shot turned to see the "weirdo" that had spouted such an announcement. I didn't care.

Before allowing myself to succumb to fear, I went into the store and boldly asked to talk to the manag-

er. (Don't bother talking to the clerks, they have no
power and for the most part they couldn't care less.
Go for the individual who has the power to do something about your complaint.) The manager came out.
I tried to keep my voice from sounding nervous and
shaky. However, my being nervous and uncomfortable
with the confrontation had nothing to do with the situation that needed to be addressed. True courage
doesn't mean the absence of fear, but rather proceeding in the face of it. I started by saying to the manager, "If this mall was a movie at a theater, it would be
rated 'R' and a person would have to be seventeen
years old to enter!!" He had no idea what I was talking
about. So, I proceeded to tell him about the picture in
front of his store that offended me. I also added an
idle threat. "If my children had been with me, you
probably would've had to call the police because I
might have torn your store apart." (I try to be nice,
but sometimes, it just doesn't happen).

He still seemed to be without a clue. I took him to
the front of the store and showed him the picture. He
was greatly apologetic and immediately took the picture down. He explained that it had likely been a
prank by one of his employees or a mischievous cus-
tomer and that the picture was never intended to be
displayed so openly. He then thanked me for my concern and assistance. I walked out of there feeling like I
had just slain a dragon. I felt invigorated. I left convinced that it's about time we, as women, who care

about the state of our home and nation, find the courage to stand up in the face of wrong and say, **"Excuse me, your butt's in the air."**

One of the consequences of women remaining silent in the face of terrible immorality has been played out in our nation's capital in recent times. One morning as I watched the impeachment hearings of President William J. Clinton, I looked on with equal parts of disgust and intense interest. In the midst of the debate, one particular statement was made that got little or no attention from the main stream media. Yet I believe it was the most damning statement I had heard to date. It was made by the Minority Leader of the House of Representatives, Richard Gephardt, and I found it to be more vile than any of the other sordid details of the Oval Office, the infamous Blue Dress, or the crimes of perjury or obstruction of justice that were discussed. Referring to the resignation of Representative Robert Livingston of Louisiana (the newly elected Speaker of the House who resigned because it was revealed that he had had numerous adulterous affairs on his wife), Richard Gephardt proposed, "Our Founding Fathers created a system of government of men, not of angels...We need to stop destroying imperfect people at the altar of an unattainable morality" (USA Today/November, 1998).

I regarded Mr. Gephardt's defense of President Clinton's and other national leaders' misconduct as ludicrous. Since when is a man's faithfulness to his wife "an unattainable morality"? Are any of us ready to teach our sons and daughters that the standard of being faithful and not having adulterous affairs is unattainable? Are we ready to admit to our husbands that striving to remain faithful and sexually exclusive to him is asking just a little too much? I was driven to scream at my television, **"Excuse me, Mr. Gephardt, your butt's in the air."** I made several phone calls to Washington that day to protest such insanity! Women have a civilizing effect on a society. When women accept perverse behavior, then the entire culture becomes corrupted. Well, here's one woman who refuses to be silenced by the evil of our time.

Whether it's at the shopping mall or the Washington Mall, may God help all of us who claim the name of Christ to be courageous enough to impact the present. Without the "salt" effect of Jesus Christ acting as preservative, our communities and our nation will rot from the inside out.

# CHAPTER
# TWELVE

As WE GRAB HOLD OF COURAGE,

WE MUST PUT OUR TRUST AND FAITH

IN THE TRUTH THAT HE IS WITH US,

NO MATTER WHAT LIES AHEAD.

# Face The Future

With the past purified by the redemptive work of Christ, and the present graced with His boldness, it is with a smile of trust in the Lord's ability to cause us to triumph that we can face whatever lies ahead.

We are given the formula for hope and courage to face the future in Matthew 14. After feeding the multitude, Jesus sent the people away and compelled the disciples to get in their boat and go across to the other side of the lake. After they were far from the shore, a raging storm came up. The battering waves and the terrible wind seemed to mark their doom. All through the night and into the early morning hours the weary disciples struggled to survive.

It was in the fourth watch, which is between 3-6 in the morning, that Jesus finally came to them, walking on the water. Not only were the disciples terrified by the storm, but they also didn't know who the approaching figure was. They perceived him as a ghost, so they cried out in fear. It was at that moment that Jesus' words to his disciples would become not only their source of comfort, but comfort to each of us throughout all time.

Before I tell you what Jesus said, it might be noteworthy to mention three things He did *not* say.

1. **"There's no storm. What is wrong with you? You are always making a mountain out of a mole hill. You are so negative."** It is a comfort to me that Jesus didn't deny the severity of the situation the disciples were in. They were going to die if Jesus didn't help them. They knew they were in trouble.

2. **"Come on guys, row harder. If you just try a little more, have a little more faith, then you can get yourself out of this mess you're in. It's your fault that you are in this storm. You just don't have the faith it takes to beat up the devil."** The disciples were in a storm, and it was not their own fault. They were in the middle of that lake…because Jesus told them to go there. Sure there are lots of times that we suffer because of our own stupidity and sin, but there are times when we are doing everything we know to do and yet the storms still come and the waves crash us down.

3. **"There's no hope, fellows, you are going to die and there's nothing you can do about it. It's just fate. You can't change the stars and it's just your time to go. Give up, there is no hope."** Jesus didn't say, "There is no storm!" He didn't say, "Row harder! And He didn't say, "Give up and die."

The words He did say are the words that help you and me stand up and face the future, no matter what is ahead. "But immediately Jesus spoke to them, saying, 'Take courage, it is I; do not be afraid'" (Matthew

14:24). That simple sentence is what gives me the courage to confront my past. I can't go back and face the hurt and the damage done to me unless and until Jesus walks with me. I cannot swim upstream against the "current" philosophies and lies of our society without Him. And I certainly cannot smile at the future unless I can look through the blinding fog of despair and see our Savior.

As I pondered the section in this account that says, "Jesus came walking through the storm at the fourth watch," I thought of the night that I was in the hospital when my 12 year-old niece was dying of Cystic Fibrosis. During the middle of the night I was talking to one of the nurses. I asked her how she dealt with the fact that all her patients were dying children. She said, "My goal is to get them through the night. I've observed that the most difficult time is right before dawn. That is when it seems to be the most critical for the children."

When she said that, I thought about Jesus appearing in the fourth watch, right before dawn, walking through the storm. I must admit, it would be my preference that Jesus' timing and method of deliverance would be a little different when it comes to the storm dilemma. I don't want Jesus to walk through the storm with me, I want Him to make it stop. I want Him to say, "Peace," and cause the waves to cease at the very first hint of a brewing wind.

Sometimes He calms the storm, but sometimes He

walks through them. Regardless of how He chooses to rescue us, His words are the same. *"Take courage."*

For some, courage comes a little easier than for others. As a small child, for example, our daughter, Heidi, was unusually timid. She didn't even like to ask for ketchup packets at McDonald's. So when Heidi shows courage, she has to work a little harder than I do. However, the command is the same for us all, regardless of personality type. We are commanded to "take courage." The rest of His words clearly answer the question, "How can we be courageous?" Jesus said, *"...Don't be afraid, because I am here."* Jesus knew that His presence was enough to give us courage to confront the past, impact the present, and to face the future.

Do you believe He is enough? That question comes to us each day and in every situation we encounter. Can we smile at the future when we are afraid there will not be enough money? Can we endure the thought of living the rest of our days without a mate? Or can we smile at the future when we face the possibility of living the rest of our lives with an insensitive, selfish spouse? Can we face the future when our teenage daughter is pregnant, or our foolish son has his girlfriend pregnant? Is it possible to face the future if God doesn't heal our diseased body?

The only way we can face the future is if Jesus will walk through the storm with us. As we grab hold of courage, we must put our trust and faith in the truth that He is with us, no matter what lies ahead.

As a parting thought about our cry for courage, let me tell you about my four most favorite gifts I have received in my lifetime. The first gift came from Steve on our very first Christmas together. That year our income was $3000 gross. (That is "gross," isn't it?) Because we had no money, there was no way he could get me a gift. Steve did, however, give me three red roses. He told me they symbolized a cord of three strands that is not easily broken (Ecclesiastes 4:12). I took a picture of the flowers and so they bloom year round. They have never faded.

My second favorite gift was given to me by our son, Nathan. That particular year he was six years old. We were into our first year of home schooling and he had learned to read. So, he gave me a little basket with some dried flowers on the lid. As I opened the lid I saw a little card inside. He had written on the card in his six-year-old printing, "Thank you for teaching me to read." I'll never forget that feeling of love and pride, when I realized that by teaching him to read, I had given him the world. He is now an honor student in college with an intense love for learning.

My third favorite gift came from my mother. We had a large family and one particular year we drew names for Christmas. Mom had gotten my name. She asked me what I wanted. I told her I wanted her to take a tape player and cassette and to tell me all about herself. I wanted her to tell me her secrets, to tell me things that she had never told anyone. She did it! And Oh! What a wonderful surprise. That tape became a great source of comfort after she died of cancer in 1996. (As a side note, Nathan took that tape and lifted off her testimony of when she became a Christian. He added the song, *It Is Well With My Soul,* which I sang at her funeral, and surprised me with it as a gift. It now appears on one of our musical CD's entitled *Chapters.* Nathan took a gift my mom had given to me and made it even more special by adding his gift to it.)

Finally, my fourth favorite gift came from our daughter, Heidi. She was four years old that memorable Christmas and had done her own shopping. As she presented her gift to me, I fought back a chuckle. She handed me a big ball of scotch tape. "Oh, Heidi, a wad of scotch tape. I love it. Thank you so much." (We mothers are so easy, don't you think?)

Heidi stood there grinning as I graciously received her offering. I started to go about my business when she said, "No, Mama, there's something inside." Sure enough, as I peeled away about twenty feet of tape, I saw a little plastic bag. It still had 99 cents on it. I opened up the bag and there it was, a little plastic baby Jesus, with a little plastic Mary and Joseph. "Oh! Heidi!" I said, "Thank you. I love this little nativity!"

However, Heidi didn't budge. She just stood there looking at me. I could tell by the hurt look on her little face that I had failed to fully grasp the incredible value of her gift. She choked back her emotions and said, "Oh, Mommy, you don't understand. Jesus glows in the dark!"

Oh! How I need the kind of Jesus that glows in the dark. I need him to come to me through the storms of life. I need Him to help me be coordinated in this life that keeps me so off balance. I've tried to keep my priorities right and they keep getting out of place. I desperately need Him with me.

I need Him to help me be content with what I have, and who I am, and with what I do.

And, by all means, I need Him to give me the courage to grab hold of His hand and allow him to walk with me through whatever I face in the years ahead…and…to help me impact the present. But perhaps the toughest challenge of all, I need Jesus to shine the light of His love on my past, to set me free from any chains that bind me. I want to be brave enough to follow the path of Psalm 139:23-24: "Search me, O God, and know my heart: try me, and know my thoughts: And see if there be any wicked way in me, and lead me in the way everlasting."

Extending the invitation to God to step into the most secret places in our heart is, by far, the most courageous act we will ever venture.

## THE SECRET PLACE

My heart is like a house
One day I let the Savior in

And there are many rooms
Where we would visit now and then
But then one day He saw that door
I knew the day had come too soon
I said, "Jesus, I'm not ready
For us to visit in that room."

"Cause that's a place in my heart
Where even I don't go
I have some things hidden there
I don't want no one to know."
But He handed me the key
With tears of love on His face
He said, "I want to make you clean,
Let me go in your secret place."

Then I opened up the door
And as the two of us walked in
I was so ashamed
His light revealed my hidden sin
But when I think about that room now
I'm not afraid anymore
Cause I know my hidden sin
No longer hides behind that door

That was a place in my heart
Where even I wouldn't go
I had some things hidden there
I didn't want no one to know
But He handed me the key

With tears of love on His face
He made me clean
I let Him in my secret place
Is there a place in your heart where even you
won't go?

(Steve Chapman/Dawn Treader Music)

\* This story was previously told in the book
*Smart Women Keep It Simple*
Bethany House Publishers
Minneapolis, Minnesota 55438
1992

\*\* This story was previously told in the book
*Running On Empty and Looking For the Nearest Exit*
Bethany House Publishers
Minneapolis, Minnesota 55438
1994

# ABOUT THE AUTHOR

Annie Chapman is an experienced communicator. Having shared the stage with her husband Steve, in musical concerts for nearly a quarter of a century, she has written several books and magazine articles. She has been featured as the keynote speaker for many women's events around the nation. After graduating from Moody Bible Institute and then marrying Steve in1975, Annie became familiar with the demands of motherhood when she gave birth to two children Nathan, in 1977 and Heidi, in 1980. Annie and Steve make their home in Pleasant View, Tennessee.

# OTHER RESOURCES FROM ANNIE CHAPMAN

## BOOKS BY ANNIE CHAPMAN (WITH MAUREEN RANK)

*Gifts Your Kids Can't Break*

*Married Lovers, Married Friends*

*Smart Women Keep It Simple*
(Bethany House Publishers)

———

## BOOKS BY ANNIE CHAPMAN

*What Do I Want?*

*Running On Empty and Looking for the Nearest Exit*
(Bethany House Publishers)

*Can I Control My Changing Emotions?* (with Shaw
and Littauer)
(Bethany House Publishers)

———

## OTHER BOOKS AVAILABLE THROUGH S & A FAMILY, INC. WRITTEN BY STEVE CHAPMAN

*A Look At Life From A Deerstand*
(Harvest House Publishers)

*Full Draw*

*Wednesday's Prayer*

*Outdoor Insights*
(Harvest House Publishers)

Much of the material in this book is available on a cassette featuring Annie Chapman in a live presentation at a Women's Conference. The cassette is entitled, "WHAT DO I WANT?"

Also:

The Song Lyrics used in this book are available on Steve and Annie Chapman's recordings

———

"THE KEY" & "THE SECRET PLACE"– recorded on FAMILY FAVORITES SACD-115 (CD only)

———

"TWO CHILDREN"– recorded on AN EVENING TOGETHER SAC-3000 (cassette only) S&A FAMILY

For a full listing of resources available for your family, contact:

S&A Family, Inc.
P.O. Box 535
Madison, TN 37116
615-385-2530
www.steveandanniechapman.com